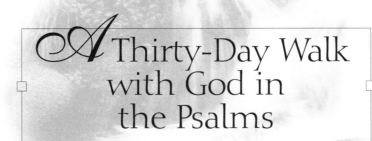

A Thirty-Day Walk with God in the Psalms

A Companion Devotional to
A Place of Quiet Rest

Nancy Leigh DeMoss

MOODY PUBLISHERS

CHICAGO

All Scripture quotations, unless otherwise indicated, are taken from the *New King James Version*. Copyright © 1979, 1980, 1982 by Thomas Nelson, Inc. Used by permission. All rights reserved.

Scripture quotations marked NIV are taken from the *Holy Bible, New International Version.*® NIV®· Copyright © 1973, 1978, 1984 by International Bible Society. Used by permission of Zondervan Publishing House. All rights reserved.

Produced with the assistance of The Livingstone Corporation. Project staff includes Paige Drygas, Chris Hudson, and Ashley Taylor.

Interior design by Design Corps.

ISBN: 0-8024-6644-3
ISBN-13: 978-0-8024-6644-0

We hope you enjoy this book from Moody Publishers. Our goal is to provide high-quality, thought-provoking books and products that connect truth to your real needs and challenges. For more information on other books and products written and produced from a biblical perspective, go to www.moodypublishers.com or write to:

Moody Publishers
820 N. LaSalle Boulevard
Chicago, IL 60610

9 10 8

Printed in the United States of America

CONTENTS

Introduction   5

How To Get the Most Out of This Study   7

PSALMS OF INSTRUCTION—A LEARNING HEART

Day One   Psalm   1   9

Day Two   Psalm   19   15

Day Three   Psalm   37   21

Day Four   Psalm   73   27

Day Five   Psalm   90   33

PSALMS OF EXPECTATION—A LEANING HEART

Day Six   Psalm   16   39

Day Seven   Psalm   23   45

Day Eight   Psalm   27   51

Day Nine   Psalm   46   57

Day Ten   Psalm   57   63

Day Eleven   Psalm   71   69

Day Twelve   Psalm   91   75

Day Thirteen   Psalm 121   81

PSALMS OF ASPIRATION—A LONGING HEART

Day Fourteen   Psalm   25   87

Day Fifteen   Psalm   42   93

Day Sixteen   Psalm   85   99

Day Seventeen   Psalm 142   105

Day Eighteen   Psalm 139   111

PSALMS OF CONTRITION—A LOWLY HEART

Day Nineteen   Psalm   32   117

Day Twenty   Psalm   51   123

Day Twenty-One   Psalm 130   129

Day Twenty-Two   Psalm 143   135

$\mathcal{P}$SALMS OF CELEBRATION—A LOVING HEART

Day Twenty-Three	Psalm 34	141
Day Twenty-Four	Psalm 36	147
Day Twenty-Five	Psalm 66	153
Day Twenty-Six	Psalm 92	159
Day Twenty-Seven	Psalm 103	165
Day Twenty-Eight	Psalm 116	171
Day Twenty-Nine	Psalm 138	177
Day Thirty	Psalm 145	183
Special Thanks To . . .		189
For More Information on Revive Our Hearts . . .		189

Without a doubt, one of the most significant influences of my childhood was the example of parents who practiced the spiritual discipline of a daily devotional life. My dad had two inviolate habits: "Spiritual food before physical food," and, "Bible reading before any other reading." This was not a legalistic practice for him; he simply believed that "man does not live by bread alone but by every word that comes from the mouth of God." He knew that this daily time alone with the Lord was his lifeline if he was to succeed as a husband and a father of seven, not to speak of juggling the demands of his business and many ministry endeavors.

Does that sound too good to be true? Do you feel too busy and overcommitted to spend your first hour alone with the Lord? Let's be honest from the beginning—it's a battle. But I am convinced it's a battle worth fighting.

In my own life, I've often struggled to make time with God my highest priority. This discipline has not always come easily for me. As much as I love my time with the Lord, I sometimes find myself fighting to make it consistent. I fight against the desire for sleep, against distractions, against sitting still, against my "to do" list, and against the enemy, who so desperately wants to see me fail.

But over the years, this habit of setting aside time alone with the Lord each day has become both an absolute necessity and an indescribable privilege. To the degree that I have made this time a priority, I have experienced incredible freedom, joy, and blessing.

In recent years, I have spoken to many Christian groups on the subject of a personal devotional life. At the end of my message, I typically ask two questions:

"How many of you would admit that you do not currently have a consistent devotional habit?" I have asked this question of thousands of people, including full-time Christian workers. Invariably, at least eighty to ninety percent of those in the room will acknowledge that they do not have a consistent quiet time. Then I ask,

"Would you be willing to make a commitment that every day for the next thirty days, you will spend at least some time alone with the Lord in the Word and in prayer?" What a joy it has been to see thousands of people take this "Thirty-Day Challenge."

Just today I received a note from a pastor's wife who was writing to thank me for challenging her to make that commitment two years ago and to tell me how her life has been transformed. Two years ago, she was a frazzled, frustrated, fragile woman. Her life today is not trouble-free, but she is growing and has a newfound hunger and heart for the Lord and His Word. She says, "I now know in reality, what it means for God's Word to be life and breath, bread and water—my sustenance—as never before."

I have discovered that many Christians believe it is important to spend time each day with the Lord, and they are willing to make that thirty-day commitment to get started, but they do not know *how* to actually spend meaningful time in the Word and in prayer.

This thirty-day devotional guide has been designed to give you a "track to run on." I have chosen thirty of my favorite psalms and provided questions and suggestions to help you explore each psalm and to make these psalms a part of your life.

The Psalms have played a vital role in my spiritual pilgrimage. Reading, studying, memorizing, meditating on, and praying through the Psalms for some forty years has taught me much about the heart and ways of God. The songs and prayers of the psalmists have helped me express the deepest joys, concerns, questions, and sorrows of my own heart to the Lord. They have tutored me in a lifestyle of praise and worship and have revealed the Lord Jesus to me.

Each of the psalms I have selected is an inexhaustible gold mine of truth. Even after mining them for years, I still keep finding riches I had previously overlooked. The studies in this collection do little more than scratch the surface. My goal is simply to whet your appetite for getting into the Word and to give you a taste of the feast that is available for those who are hungry to know Him through His Word.

So for the next thirty days, I invite you to take a walk—to find a quiet place and time each day, to open your Bible and your heart, and to know, worship, and enjoy God in a fresh way. I guarantee you'll never be quite the same.

Nancy Leigh DeMoss

1. If you have not already done so, *begin by taking the "Thirty-Day Challenge."* Purpose in your heart that for the next thirty days, you will spend some time every day alone with the Lord, in His Word and in prayer. Share your commitment with another believer who will encourage you and help hold you accountable. (You may want to invite one or more friends to make the same commitment and to work through their own copies of this book. You may also want to meet together on the phone or in person each week to share how the Lord is speaking to each of you through your personal time with Him.)

2. Having made a thirty-day commitment, *determine when and where you plan to meet with the Lord each day.* Ask the Lord to direct you in this matter. Make an "appointment" with the Lord, much as you would schedule a doctor's appointment or some other important engagement. If at all possible, I would encourage you to make this your first meeting of each day. (That may also mean a commitment to get to bed earlier at night.) Regardless, set aside some time—morning, afternoon, or evening—to spend alone with the Lord. Do everything you can to keep your appointment with Him. However, if you are unavoidably interrupted, don't put yourself on a guilt trip. Find another time in the day.

3. *Read the passage on your own* and allow God to speak to you before you start answering the questions I have suggested. You will notice that the psalms are not written out in this book. That is to encourage you to read and study out of your own Bible.

4. *Don't feel you have to answer every question.* Your goal is not to fill in all the blanks but to meet with God—not to have "devotions," but to have "devotion." The questions have been provided to help you get into the Word and get the Word into you. If you are unable to answer all the questions in the available time, then just select one or more questions from each section:

- ↝ *What does this passage say?* (Observation)

- ↝ *What does it mean?* (Interpretation)

- ↝ *How can I make it a part of my life?* (Application)

Make sure you don't spend your entire devotional time filling in the blanks. Include time for meditation, praise, and prayer. Feel free to be spontaneous. If you sense the Lord leading you to spend your entire time in one section, then follow His leading, not the journal.

5. *Sing to the Lord. (Aloud!)* The Book of Psalms includes nearly seventy references to singing to the Lord. You may not think you have a good singing voice, but there is something wonderfully freeing about singing openly before your Father.

At the end of each study, you will find the lyrics to a hymn or song that relates to the message of the psalm for that day. There are many contemporary choruses and songs that could have been chosen. However, I have intentionally selected songs that have survived the test of time and have been sung by God's people for a generation or longer. My hope is that these hymns and songs will remain a part of the devotional literature and the praise and worship of God's people for generations to come. For those who may be unfamiliar with the tunes to these hymns, they can be found in most standard hymnals. A hymnal can become a wonderful devotional aid for your times of praise.

6. *Don't rush through this book.* You don't have to finish it in thirty days. If you want to spend two or more days working through particular psalms, that's fine. Remember your objective: to get to know God.

7. *If you miss a day, don't give up.* Start again the next day. The enemy knows that the habit of a daily meeting with the Lord will change your life, and he will do everything he can to discourage or defeat you. Don't let him have that victory.

8. *Once you have completed your "Thirty-Day Challenge"—don't stop!* I pray that after thirty days of meeting with the Lord, you will be hungry for more and will want to make this a lifetime habit.[1] For now, though, don't feel intimidated. Just look forward to your time with the Lord over the next thirty days.

---

[1] *A Place of Quiet Rest: Finding Intimacy With God Through a Daily Devotional Life,* by Nancy Leigh DeMoss (Chicago: Moody Press, 2000), includes many practical insights about how to develop a daily devotional life.

Psalm 1

Preparing Your Heart

Ask God to quiet your heart and to speak to you through His Word. Ask Him to shine the light of His truth into your life. In this quiet moment, surrender yourself to Him and commit to obey whatever He shows you. Begin your time of devotion with this prayer:

> *Open my eyes that I may see*
> *wonderful things in your law.*
> *Give me understanding, and I will keep your law*
> *and obey it with all my heart.*
> *Show me your ways, O Lord,*
> *teach me your paths;*
> *guide me in your truth and teach me,*
> *for you are God my Savior,*
> *and my hope is in you all day long.*
> *Teach me what I cannot see;*
> *if I have done wrong, I will not do so again.*
>
> PSALM 119:18, 34; 25:4–5; JOB 34:32 NIV

*L*istening to God

∞ Read Psalm 1 thoughtfully and prayerfully.

∞ What key words stand out to you in this passage?

∞ Write out a key verse from this passage.

∞ Summarize the entire passage in a sentence or two.

WHAT DOES THIS PASSAGE SAY?
(Observation)

"This psalm may be regarded as The Preface Psalm, having in it a notification of the contents of the entire Book. It is the Psalmist's desire to teach us the way to blessedness and to warn us of the sure destruction of sinners. This, then, is the matter of the First Psalm, which may be looked upon, in some respects, as the text upon which the whole of the Psalms make up a divine sermon."[1]

CHARLES H. SPURGEON

1. What are the characteristics of a righteous person? What does he avoid? What does he love to think about (vv. 1–2)?

_____

_____

2. How does the word picture of a "transplanted tree" describe the righteous (v. 3)?

_____

_____

"Trees do not plant themselves; neither do sinful people transport themselves into God's kingdom. Salvation is His marvelous work of grace. Yet, there is genuine responsibility in appropriating the abundant resources of God, which lead to eventual productivity."[2]

JOHN MACARTHUR

3. What words are used to refer to evildoers in this psalm (vv. 1, 4)? What insights do those words give you into the unrighteous?

_____

_____

FOR FURTHER INSIGHT

"The picture is that of a threshing floor on a hill-top, where the wind clears away the chaff and leaves the grain."[3]

4. Compare the first word of this psalm with the last word. What do these two words reveal about the outcome of the righteous and of the ungodly?

_____

_____

WHAT DOES THIS PASSAGE MEAN?
(Interpretation)

1. How can we be secure, fruitful, consistent, and prosperous in our Christian walk?

_____

_____

2. How do people's choices, lifestyles, and appetites reveal the true condition of their hearts?

_____

3. If an individual is drawn toward ungodly people and influences, does not have an appetite for the Word of God, and is not living a spiritually fruitful life, what does that suggest about his spiritual condition?

4. What does it mean to meditate on the law of God?

HOW CAN I MAKE THIS PASSAGE A PART OF MY LIFE?
(Application)

1. What do your choices, interests, and priorities reveal about your heart?

2. Are there areas of your life where you are choosing to expose yourself to ungodly input?

3. Are you more influenced by the thinking and lifestyles of ungodly people ·or by meditation on the Word of God?

4. How can you cultivate a greater hunger for and delight in God's Word? How can you make His Word a greater part of your life?

_____

_____

FOR FURTHER MEDITATION

James 1:21–25

ℛesponding to God

PRAISE

What does this passage reveal to you about God and His ways? Praise Him for His Word and for what it has meant in your life.

_____

_____

_____

PRAYER

Confession: Agree with God about any areas where you may have adopted ungodly ways of thinking or living.

Supplication: Ask God to give you a greater love and hunger for His Word.

Intercession: Use this passage as a basis to pray for someone whom God places on your heart.

SING TO THE LORD

Trust and Obey

When we walk with the Lord in the light of His Word,
What a glory He sheds on our way!
While we do His good will, He abides with us still,
And with all who will trust and obey.

> Trust and obey, for there's no other way
> To be happy in Jesus, but to trust and obey.

Not a shadow can rise, not a cloud in the skies,
But His smile quickly drives it away;
Not a doubt nor a fear, not a sigh nor a tear
Can abide while we trust and obey.

But we never can prove the delights of His love
Until all on the altar we lay;
For the favor He shows and the joy He bestows
Are for them who will trust and obey.

Then in fellowship sweet we will sit at His feet,
Or we'll walk by His side in the way;
What He says we will do, where He sends we will go;
Never fear, only trust and obey.

JOHN H. SAMMIS

TAKE-AWAY THOUGHT

*What key thought, phrase, or verse from this psalm
will you take with you into your day?*

[1] Charles H. Spurgeon, *The Treasury of David* (Grand Rapids: Kregel Publications, 1968), 13.

[2] John MacArthur, *The MacArthur Study Bible* (Nashville: Word Bibles, 1997), 743.

[3] Charles F. Pfeiffer and Everett F. Harrison, ed., *The Wycliffe Bible Commentary* (Chicago: Moody Press, 1990), 496.

Psalm 19

Preparing Your Heart

Ask God to quiet your heart and to speak to you through His Word. Ask Him to shine the light of His truth into your life. In this quiet moment, surrender yourself to Him and commit to obey whatever He shows you. Begin your time of devotion with this prayer:

> Open my eyes that I may see
>   wonderful things in your law.
> Give me understanding, and I will keep your law
>   and obey it with all my heart.
> Show me your ways, O Lord,
>   teach me your paths;
> guide me in your truth and teach me,
>   for you are God my Savior,
>   and my hope is in you all day long.
> Teach me what I cannot see;
>   if I have done wrong, I will not do so again.
>
> PSALM 119:18, 34; 25:4–5; JOB 34:32 NIV

$\mathcal{L}$istening to God

- Read Psalm 19 thoughtfully and prayerfully.

- What key words stand out to you in this passage?

- Write out a key verse from this passage.

- Summarize the entire passage in a sentence or two.

WHAT DOES THIS PASSAGE SAY?
(Observation)

The psalmist (David) marvels at two ways that God has revealed Himself to humanity:

Natural (general) revelation (vv. 1–6)

1. What does creation tell us about God?

_____

_____

_____

_____

"Though all preachers on earth should grow silent, and every human mouth cease from publishing the glory of God, the heavens above will never cease to declare and proclaim His majesty and glory."[1]

AUGUSTUS T. THOLUCK

Special (specific) revelation (vv. 7–11)

2. What is the connection between "the heavens" (vv. 1–6) and "the law of the LORD" (vv. 7–11)?

_____

_____

3. What synonyms are used in this passage for the Word of God (vv. 7–9)? What adjectives are used to describe the Word of God (vv. 7–9)?

_____

_____

4. David's response in the light of God's revelation was *self-examination* (vv. 12–14). What two kinds of sins does the psalmist pray to be delivered from (vv. 12–13)?

_____

_____

5. What does he want the Word of God to accomplish in his life?

_____

_____

WHAT DOES THIS PASSAGE MEAN?
(Interpretation)

1. Why is the Word of God so vital and valuable to the child of God?

_____

17

2. God promises "great reward" to those who "keep" His Word (v. 11). What does it mean to keep His Word?

_____

_____

3. Why is God's Word more valuable than our most precious possessions and sweeter than the greatest pleasures on this earth?

_____

_____

4. Many people think of obeying God's law as a burden. Why is it more a privilege and a blessing than a burden?

_____

_____

HOW CAN I MAKE THIS PASSAGE A PART OF MY LIFE?
(Application)

1. What are some specific areas of your life that have been changed by the Word of God?

_____

_____

2. Which of the benefits and blessings in verses 7–11 would you like to experience in greater measure?

_____

_____

3. What practical steps can you take to make the Word a higher priority in your life?

4. Are you aware of anything in the Word of God that you are not currently obeying? Will you repent of going your own way and begin walking in obedience to His Word?

FOR FURTHER MEDITATION
2 Timothy 3:14–17

$\mathcal{R}$esponding to God

PRAISE

Thank God for His Word. Thank Him for making it available to you, and praise Him for the way that His Word has blessed and protected your life.

PRAYER

Confession: Admit any hidden or willful sins that God reveals as you ask Him to search and cleanse your heart.

Supplication: Pray the prayer of verses 12–14 in your own words.

Intercession: Use this passage as a basis to pray for someone whom God places on your heart.

SING TO THE LORD

Break Thou the Bread of Life

Break Thou the bread of life, dear Lord, to me,
As thou didst break the loaves beside the sea;
Beyond the sacred page, I seek Thee, Lord;
My spirit pants for Thee, O Living Word.

Break Thou the bread of life, O Lord, to me,
That hid within my heart Thy Word may be;
Mold Thou each inward thought, from self set free,
And let my steps be all controlled by Thee.

Open the Word of Truth that I may see
Thy message written clear and plain for me;
Then in sweet fellowship, walking with Thee,
Thine image on my life engraved will be.

MARY A. LATHBURY

ALEXANDER GROVES, LAST STANZA

TAKE-AWAY THOUGHT

*What key thought, phrase, or verse from this psalm
will you take with you into your day?*

[1] Spurgeon, *Treasury of David*, 86.

Psalm 37

*P*reparing Your Heart

Ask God to quiet your heart and to speak to you through His Word. Ask Him to shine the light of His truth into your life. In this quiet moment, surrender yourself to Him and commit to obey whatever He shows you. Begin your time of devotion with this prayer:

> *Open my eyes that I may see*
> *wonderful things in your law.*
> *Give me understanding, and I will keep your law*
> *and obey it with all my heart.*
> *Show me your ways, O Lord,*
> *teach me your paths;*
> *guide me in your truth and teach me,*
> *for you are God my Savior,*
> *and my hope is in you all day long.*
> *Teach me what I cannot see;*
> *if I have done wrong, I will not do so again.*
>
> PSALM 119:18, 34; 25:4–5; JOB 34:32 NIV

$\mathscr{L}$istening to God

- Read Psalm 37 thoughtfully and prayerfully.
- What key words stand out to you in this passage?

- Write out a key verse from this passage.

- Summarize the entire passage in a sentence or two.

WHAT DOES THIS PASSAGE SAY?
(Observation)

1. This psalm deals with a difficult issue that God's people in every generation have had to face. In your own words, what is that challenge?

_____

_____

2. As in Psalm 1, two kinds of people are considered in this passage. The wicked and the righteous are contrasted in terms of their character, their lifestyle, and the ultimate outcome of their lives. Read through Psalm 37 again and make a note of the following:

   Words or phrases used to refer to or describe the wicked:

   Outcome of the wicked:

   Words or phrases used to refer to or describe the righteous:

Outcome of the righteous:

WHAT DOES THIS PASSAGE MEAN?
(Interpretation)

People who live ungodly lives often prosper, while those who try to obey God are afflicted. Psalm 37 does not really provide an explanation for this seeming injustice. Rather, it challenges the believer to view this reality in light of eternity and to respond in faith.

1. How should we *not* respond to the behavior and apparent well-being of the ungodly? (What negative command is repeated in verses 1, 7, 8?)

_____

_____

_____

Spotlight on a Word

The word translated fret suggests more than simply being worried or bothered. It means "to glow or grow warm; figuratively to blaze up, of anger, zeal, jealousy; to be angry, burn, be displeased, grieve, be incensed, be wroth";[1] to "grow indignant."[2] Verse eight shows the connection between fretting and anger and reminds us that fretting "only leads to harm."

2. How *should* we respond when the wicked do wicked things and prosper while we suffer and struggle? (Look for the positive commands in verses 3–8, 27, 34.)

_____

_____

_____

"Resting in the Lord does not depend on external circumstances at all, but on your relationship to God Himself."[3]

OSWALD CHAMBERS

3. The difference between the two responses is a matter of our focus. Where is our focus when we are fretting? Where is our focus when we are responding as we should?

---

4. What phrases in this psalm exhort us to keep our focus on the Lord (vv. 3–5, 7, 9, 34, 40)?

---

5. How does an "eternal perspective" affect the way we view this earthly life? How does looking at life from the perspective of eternity help us endure hardships?

HOW CAN I MAKE THIS PASSAGE A PART OF MY LIFE?
(Application)

1. When have you fretted over the behavior or lifestyle of an ungodly person (or group of people)?

---

2. Oswald Chambers says, "Fretting springs from a determination to get our own way. . . . All our fret and worry is caused by calculating without God."[4] How do you see this truth played out in your life?

---

3. What people or circumstances in your life are you trying to change or "fix"? Consciously turn them over to God right now, and purpose to take your hands off each situation.

---

4. When have you had to wait for God's answer or solution? How did the process of waiting benefit you?

FOR FURTHER MEDITATION
Matthew 5:3–10; Galatians 6:9; Hebrews 10:36–37

$\mathcal{R}$esponding to God

PRAISE

Personalize the promises God makes to the righteous in this passage (from vv. 4, 11, 23–24, 28, 31, 33, 34, 37, 40) and thank Him for them.

PRAYER

Confession: Release any fretting or anger that is in your heart toward your circumstances or toward other people. Confess any failure on your part to "rest in the Lord and wait patiently for Him" (v. 7).

Supplication: Ask God to give you an eternal perspective that will help you to trust in Him, delight in Him, commit your way to Him, rest in Him, and wait on Him.

Intercession: Use this passage as a basis to pray for someone whom God places on your heart.

SING TO THE LORD

Be Still My Soul

Be still, my soul! The Lord is on thy side;
Bear patiently the cross of grief or pain.
Leave to thy God to order and provide;
In every change He faithful will remain.
Be still, my soul! Thy best, thy heav'nly Friend
Thro' thorny ways leads to a joyful end.

Be still, my soul! Thy God doth undertake
To guide the future as He has the past.
Thy hope, thy confidence let nothing shake;
All now mysterious shall be bright at last.
Be still, my soul! The waves and winds still know
His voice who ruled them while He dwelt below.

Be still, my soul! The hour is hast'ning on
When we shall be forever with the Lord,
When disappointment, grief, and fear are gone,
Sorrow forgot, love's purest joys restored.
Be still, my soul! When change and tears are past,
All safe and blessed we shall meet at last.

KATHARINA VON SCHLEGEL
TRANSLATED BY JANE L. BORTHWICK

TAKE-AWAY THOUGHT

What key thought, phrase, or verse from this psalm
will you take with you into your day?

[1] James Strong, "Hebrew and Chaldee Dictionary" in *Strong's Exhaustive Concordance*, Compact Edition (Grand Rapids: Baker Book House, 1982), 43.

[2] *The Complete Word Study Old Testament* (Chattanooga: AMG Publishers, 1994), 2318.

[3] Oswald Chambers, *My Utmost for His Highest: Selections for the Year* (Ulrichsville, OH: Barbour Publishing, Inc., 1997), July 4.

[4] Ibid.

Psalm 73

Preparing Your Heart

Ask God to quiet your heart and to speak to you through His Word. Ask Him to shine the light of His truth into your life. In this quiet moment, surrender yourself to Him and commit to obey whatever He shows you. Begin your time of devotion with this prayer:

> Open my eyes that I may see
>   wonderful things in your law.
> Give me understanding, and I will keep your law
>   and obey it with all my heart.
> Show me your ways, O Lord,
>   teach me your paths;
> guide me in your truth and teach me,
>   for you are God my Savior,
>   and my hope is in you all day long.
> Teach me what I cannot see;
>   if I have done wrong, I will not do so again.

PSALM 119:18, 34; 25:4–5; JOB 34:32 NIV

𝒮istening to God

🐌 Read Psalm 73 thoughtfully and prayerfully.

🐌 What key words stand out to you in this passage?

🐌 Write out a key verse from this passage.

🐌 Summarize the entire passage in a sentence or two.

WHAT DOES THIS PASSAGE SAY?
(Observation)

"Asaph was a Levite who led one of the temple choirs (1 Chron 15:19; 25:1–2). His name is identified with Ps 73–83, and also Ps 50. He either wrote these psalms, or his choir sang them, or later choirs in the tradition of Asaph sang them."[1]

JOHN MACARTHUR

1. How would you summarize the problem the psalmist addresses in this psalm?

_____

_____

2. What caused the psalmist to doubt the goodness of God, which he had once affirmed so confidently?

_____

_____

3. This psalm suggests three major stages in the psalmist's thinking. The progression is indicated by his use of pronouns.

(vv. 3–12) How many times do the words *they, their,* or *them* appear? Who is the object of the psalmist's focus in these verses? What is the result?

_____

(vv. 13–22) How many times do the words *I, me,* and *my* appear? Who is the object of the psalmist's focus? What is the result?

_____

(vv. 23–28) Count every use of the words *You* and *Your (Thee/Thy* KJV). Who is the psalmist's focus in this final section? What is the result?

_____

_____

4. What consequences does the psalmist experience as a result of comparing himself to the wicked (vv. 2, 21–22)?

_____

_____

5. What verse is the turning point in the psalmist's struggle? Where was the psalmist finally able to get the proper perspective on his struggle?

_____

_____

6. What blessings did the psalmist have that the wicked will never have (vv. 23–26)?

_____

_____

WHAT DOES THIS PASSAGE MEAN?
(Interpretation)

1. How does nearness to God help us maintain a proper perspective on the seemingly trouble-free lives of many people who do not walk with God?

_____

_____

> *"But when the pure in heart, those blessed ones, shall see God (Matt 5:8), they will not say that they cleansed their hearts in vain."[2]*
>
> MATTHEW HENRY

2. Why is comparison so deadly and destructive?

_____

_____

3. In the midst of his doubts, why did the psalmist determine not to tell others about his struggles (v. 15)?

_____

_____

4. What do the righteous have to look forward to? How might earthly adversity contribute to eternal prosperity?

_____

_____

HOW CAN I MAKE THIS PASSAGE A PART OF MY LIFE?
(Application)

1. Have you ever struggled, as the psalmist did, with the feeling that it doesn't pay to obey God? Describe the circumstances that made you feel that way.

_____

_____

_____

2. Do you ever verbalize your thoughts in a way that could cause other believers to doubt the goodness of God? Do your words tend to ignite faith in the hearts of other believers or give them reason to doubt the goodness of God?

_____

_____

3. What insights from this psalm provide encouragement to persevere, even in times of trouble?

_____

_____

4. Try to personalize the prayer of verses 25–26. Write out your heartfelt response to God.

_____

_____

FOR FURTHER MEDITATION

Hebrews 12:5a–8, 11

*R*esponding to God

PRAISE

Thank God for His goodness, in spite of any circumstances in your life that may have caused you to doubt that He is good.

PRAYER

⚭ *Confession:* Admit any tendencies you have had to question the goodness of God, to covet the prosperity of others, or to resent God's chastening in your life.

⚭ *Supplication:* Ask God to help you desire His nearness more than you desire anything else in heaven or on earth. Express your desire to trust Him in the midst of adversity.

⚭ *Intercession:* Use this passage as a basis to pray for someone whom God places on your heart.

SING TO THE LORD

Day by Day and With Each Passing Moment

Day by day and with each passing moment,
Strength I find to meet my trials here.
Trusting in my Father's wise bestowment,
I've no cause for worry or for fear.
He whose heart is kind beyond all measure,
Gives unto each day what He deems best,
Lovingly its part of pain and pleasure,
Mingling toil with peace and rest.

Every day the Lord Himself is near me
With a special mercy for each hour.
All my cares He fain would bear and cheer me,
He whose name is Counselor and Pow'r.

The protection of His child and treasure
Is a charge that on Himself He laid.
"As your days, your strength shall be in measure,"
This the pledge to me He made.

Help me then in every tribulation
So to trust Your promises, O Lord,
That I lose not faith's sweet consolation
Offered me within Your holy Word.
Help me, Lord, when toil and trouble meeting,
E'er to take, as from a Father's hand,
One by one, the days, the moments fleeting,
Till I reach the Promised Land.

CAROLINA SANDELL BERG
TRANSLATED BY ANDRES L. SKOOG

TAKE-AWAY THOUGHT

*What key thought, phrase, or verse from this psalm
will you take with you into your day?*

---

1 *MacArthur Study Bible*, 806.
2 Matthew Henry, *Commentary on the Whole Bible*, ed. Rev. Leslie F. Church (Grand Rapids: Zondervan, 1960), 655.

Psalm 90

Preparing Your Heart

Ask God to quiet your heart and to speak to you through His Word. Ask Him to shine the light of His truth into your life. In this quiet moment, surrender yourself to Him and commit to obey whatever He shows you. Begin your time of devotion with this prayer:

> *Open my eyes that I may see*
> *wonderful things in your law.*
> *Give me understanding, and I will keep your law*
> *and obey it with all my heart.*
> *Show me your ways, O Lord,*
> *teach me your paths;*
> *guide me in your truth and teach me,*
> *for you are God my Savior,*
> *and my hope is in you all day long.*
> *Teach me what I cannot see;*
> *if I have done wrong, I will not do so again.*
>
> PSALM 119:18, 34; 25:4–5; JOB 34:32 NIV

$\mathscr{L}$istening to God

∞ Read Psalm 90 thoughtfully and prayerfully.

∞ What key words stand out to you in this passage?

∞ Write out a key verse from this passage.

∞ Summarize the entire passage in a sentence or two.

WHAT DOES THIS PASSAGE SAY?
(Observation)

Understanding the Setting

Psalm 90 is "a prayer of Moses the man of God." Moses led God's people as they wandered in the wilderness for forty years; he watched as nearly two million adults perished under the judgment of God—an average of seventy funerals every day! In his prayer, Moses ponders the brevity, frailty, and sinfulness of people, the fierceness of God's wrath, and the meaning of these few days on earth in the light of God's eternity. He realizes that only by God's mercy can the otherwise meaningless labor and sorrow of life on this planet be turned into something of significance and joy.

1. Moses begins his prayer by worshiping God. What is the primary attribute of God that he praises (vv. 1–2)?

_____

_____

2. What contrasts does this passage make between God and humanity (vv. 1–11)?

_____

_____

3. What images does Moses use to describe the frailty and brevity of our earthly existence (vv. 3–6)?

_____

_____

"Here is the history of the grass—sown, grown, blown, mown, gone; and the history of man is not much more. . . . Glass is granite compared with flesh; and vapors are rocks compared with life."[1]

CHARLES H. SPURGEON

4. In light of humanity's plight, what is the psalmist's conclusion (v. 12)?

_____

_____

5. What requests does Moses make of God, in light of all he has observed about life (vv. 12–17)?

_____

_____

WHAT DOES THIS PASSAGE MEAN?
(Interpretation)

1. What can transform a lifetime of "labor and sorrow" (v. 10) into something of meaning and beauty?

2. The psalmist says that God is the "dwelling place" of His people. How does that "eternal home" compare with the living conditions of the Israelites while they were in the wilderness?

HOW CAN I MAKE THIS PASSAGE A PART OF MY LIFE?
(Application)

1. How can recognizing God as your "dwelling place" affect your perspective on your physical surroundings and your earthly relationships?

"God is our sanctuary for protection, sustenance, and stability."[2]

JOHN MACARTHUR

2. Calculate approximately how many days you have already lived. If God gives you a lifespan of 70 years (25,550 days), how many days do you have left on earth? How do you want to live those remaining days?

3. What practical difference would it make for you to live your life "in the light of eternity"?

_____

_____

FOR FURTHER MEDITATION
2 Peter 3:8–13

 _R_esponding to God

PRAISE

What does this passage reveal to you about God and His ways? Praise Him for His mercy that makes your life more than simply "labor and sorrow."

PRAYER

Confession: "You have set our iniquities before You, our secret sins in the light of Your countenance" (v. 8). Ask God to illuminate the secret places of your heart. Confess any hidden sins He reveals.

Supplication: Ask God to teach you to number your days and to live your life wisely in light of the brevity of life, the certainty of death, and the reality of eternity. Personalize the requests in verses 12–17.

Intercession: Use this passage as a basis to pray for someone whom God places on your heart.

SING TO THE LORD

O God, Our Help in Ages Past

O God, our Help in ages past, our Hope for years to come,
Our shelter from the stormy blast, and our eternal Home!

Under the shadow of Thy throne still may we dwell secure;
Sufficient is Thine arm alone, and our defense is sure.

Before the hills in order stood, or earth received her frame,
From everlasting Thou art God, to endless years the same.

A thousand ages in Thy sight are like an evening gone;
Short as the watch that ends the night before the rising sun.

O God, our Help in ages past, our Hope for years to come,
Be Thou our Guide while life shall last, and our eternal Home.

ISAAC WATTS

TAKE-AWAY THOUGHT

*What key thought, phrase, or verse from this psalm
will you take with you into your day?*

---

[1] Spurgeon, *Treasury of David*, 378–379.

[2] *MacArthur Study Bible*, 823.

Psalm 16

♥ Preparing Your Heart

Ask God to quiet your heart and to speak to you through His Word. Ask Him to shine the light of His truth into your life. In this quiet moment, surrender yourself to Him and commit to obey whatever He shows you. Begin your time of devotion with this prayer:

> *Open my eyes that I may see*
> *   wonderful things in your law.*
> *Give me understanding, and I will keep your law*
> *   and obey it with all my heart.*
> *Show me your ways, O Lord,*
> *   teach me your paths;*
> *guide me in your truth and teach me,*
> *   for you are God my Savior,*
> *   and my hope is in you all day long.*
> *Teach me what I cannot see;*
> *   if I have done wrong, I will not do so again.*
>
> PSALM 119:18, 34; 25:4–5; JOB 34:32 NIV

$\mathscr{L}$istening to God

- Read Psalm 16 thoughtfully and prayerfully.

- What key words stand out to you in this passage?

- Write out a key verse from this passage.

- Summarize the entire passage in a sentence or two.

WHAT DOES THIS PASSAGE SAY?
(Observation)

1. To take refuge in someone implies exclusive trust—that there is no other person or place where you could find greater safety. In whom has David taken refuge (v. 1)?

_____

_____

2. To whom did David attribute any goodness in his life (v. 2)?

_____

_____

What's in a Name?

In verse two, notice the variation of the spelling between "LORD" and "Lord." (The difference is in the capitalization.) LORD is the proper name for God most often used in the Old Testament—literally translated "The Lord God Jehovah." Lord is a title that means "Master." David's statement could be rendered, "I said to the Lord God Jehovah, 'You are my Master.'"

3. David said he took delight in a particular group of people. Who were they (v. 3)?

_____

_____

4. David looked at another group of people and fully expected them to experience great sorrow. What was the identifying characteristic of those people (v. 4)?

_____

_____

5. Why did David not feel the need or desire to pursue the false gods of his day (vv. 5–6, 11)?

_____

_____

6. David said he had "set the LORD always before [him]." What are some of the benefits he enjoyed as a result (vv. 7–11)?

_____

_____

WHAT DOES THIS PASSAGE MEAN?
(Interpretation)

1. What are some of the false gods that are common in our culture?

_____

_____

2. What sorrows might someone experience as a result of following after these gods?

_____

_____

3. What are some of the ways people try to find joy and fulfillment?

_____

_____

4. According to this psalm, what is the only source of true, lasting joy?

_____

_____

5. In his message on the Day of Pentecost, the Apostle Peter quoted verses 8–11 of this psalm and explained that David was speaking of Christ. According to Acts 2:22–31, how was this psalm fulfilled in the Lord Jesus? How does this promise also apply to those who have trusted in Christ?

_____

_____

_____

HOW CAN I MAKE THIS PASSAGE A PART OF MY LIFE?
(Application)

1. David purposed not to even speak of the false gods that others worshiped. Do you ever speak in approving ways about things that God has condemned?

_____

_____

2. What "idols" or "gods" in your life distract you from following God? What consequences have you experienced for your loyalty to other gods?

_____

_____

3. What does it mean to delight in other believers? What are some practical ways you can demonstrate and express your love for your brothers and sisters in the Lord?

_____

_____

4. The things we think about during the day greatly influence the subconscious thought patterns of our sleep. (See v. 7.) What are some things you can do to keep God primary in your thoughts throughout the day?

_____

_____

FOR FURTHER MEDITATION
2 Corinthians 5:5–9

*R*esponding to God

PRAISE

Personalize David's praise in verses 5–11 and make it your own. Praise God for your "inheritance"—the present and future blessings that are yours in Christ.

43

PRAYER

∽ *Confession:*   Agree with God about any false gods that have distracted you from wholehearted devotion to Him.

∽ *Supplication:*   Ask the Lord to give you a contented, trusting heart—one that is satisfied with Him and His provision.

∽ *Intercession:*   Use this passage as a basis to pray for someone whom God places on your heart.

SING TO THE LORD

Be Thou My Vision

Be Thou my Vision, O Lord of my heart;
Naught be all else to me, save that Thou art—
Thou my best thought, by day or by night,
Waking or sleeping, Thy presence my light.

Riches I heed not, nor man's empty praise,
Thou mine inheritance, now and always;
Thou and Thou only, first in my heart,
High King of heaven, my treasure Thou art.

High King of heaven, my victory won,
May I reach heaven's joys, bright heaven's Sun!
Heart of my own heart, whatever befall,
Still be my Vision, O Ruler of all. [1]

TAKE-AWAY THOUGHT

What key thought, phrase, or verse from this psalm
will you take with you into your day?

[1] Traditional Irish hymn, Mary E. Byrne, trans.

Psalm 23

Preparing Your Heart

Ask God to quiet your heart and to speak to you through His Word. Ask Him to shine the light of His truth into your life. In this quiet moment, surrender yourself to Him and commit to obey whatever He shows you. Begin your time of devotion with this prayer:

> *Open my eyes that I may see*
> *wonderful things in your law.*
> *Give me understanding, and I will keep your law*
> *and obey it with all my heart.*
> *Show me your ways, O Lord,*
> *teach me your paths;*
> *guide me in your truth and teach me,*
> *for you are God my Savior,*
> *and my hope is in you all day long.*
> *Teach me what I cannot see;*
> *if I have done wrong, I will not do so again.*
>
> PSALM 119:18, 34; 25:4–5; JOB 34:32 NIV

ℒistening to God

- Read Psalm 23 thoughtfully and prayerfully.

- What key words stand out to you in this passage?

- Write out a key verse from this passage.

- Summarize the entire passage in a sentence or two.

WHAT DOES THIS PASSAGE SAY?
(Observation)

This psalm is perhaps the best-known passage in the Old Testament. David uses two images to describe his relationship with the Lord:

A sheep in the care of a devoted shepherd (vv. 1–4)

> "*Sheep cannot survive alone in the wild, but must always be in the company of a shepherd. The Middle Eastern shepherd loved his sheep, gave each one a name, and cared for each one tenderly. Many a shepherd interposed himself between wild beasts and his sheep, and at night the shepherd lay down and slept in the single doorway to his sheepfold. Any enemy would have to pass him to attack his flock.*"[1]
>
> LAWRENCE O. RICHARDS

What phrases speak of the Lord as our . . .

- Nurturer?

- Provider?

- Guide?

- Protector?

- Companion?

A guest in the home of a gracious host (vv. 5–6)

> "In the Middle East, hospitality was greatly valued. The needs of a guest were gladly supplied, even if the family of the host had to go without as the price of generosity. A person who had taken a meal in one's home was assured of the protection of his host. Even an enemy, once served a meal, was totally secure for as long as his visit should last."[2]
>
> LAWRENCE O. RICHARDS

What words would you use to describe the "hospitality" offered by the Lord?

_____

_____

WHAT DOES THIS PASSAGE MEAN?
(Interpretation)

1. What difference did knowing God as his Shepherd and his Host make in David's life?

   In relation to his past?

   _____

   _____

   In relation to the present?

   _____

   _____

   In relation to his future?

   _____

   _____

2. Does having Christ as our Shepherd mean we will never have unfulfilled desires? What is the meaning of "I shall not want"?

_____

_____

_____

> *"I shall be supplied with whatever I need; and, if I have not everything I desire, I may conclude it is either not fit for me or not good for me, or I shall have it in due time."*[3]
>
> MATTHEW HENRY

HOW CAN I MAKE THIS PASSAGE A PART OF MY LIFE?
(Application)

1. What are some of the means the Good Shepherd uses to meet these basic spiritual needs in the lives of His sheep?

    Nourishment and refreshment (1 Peter 2:2; Jeremiah 15:16; Psalm 16:11)

_____

_____

Restoration (Revelation 3:19; Hebrews 12:12–13; Galatians 6:1)

_____

_____

Guidance (Psalm 119:105; Romans 8:14)

_____

_____

Protection (Psalm 119:11; Ephesians 6:10–18)

_____

_____

2. Which of these needs are you facing at this time? What changes can you make so that you rely fully on God to meet that need?

_____

_____

FOR FURTHER MEDITATION
John 10:11, 14, 27–28; Hebrews 13:20–21

$\mathcal{R}$esponding to God

PRAISE

Pray through this psalm aloud, personalizing each phrase from your heart to the Lord, and thanking Him for the reality of each of these truths and promises in your life.

PRAYER

Confession: Acknowledge any areas where you have been resisting rather than following your Shepherd.

Supplication: Ask the Lord to give you a trusting, submissive heart toward Him. Ask Him to meet all your needs.

Intercession: Use this passage as a basis to pray for someone whom God places on your heart.

SING TO THE LORD

Savior, Like a Shepherd Lead Us

Savior, like a shepherd lead us, much we need Thy tender care;
In Thy pleasant pastures feed us, for our use Thy folds prepare:
Blessed Jesus, blessed Jesus, Thou hast bought us, Thine we are;
Blessed Jesus, blessed Jesus, Thou hast bought us, Thine we are.

We are Thine, do Thou befriend us, be the Guardian of our way;
Keep Thy flock, from sin defend us, seek us when we go astray:
Blessed Jesus, blessed Jesus, hear, O hear us when we pray;
Blessed Jesus, blessed Jesus, hear, O hear us when we pray.

HYMNS FOR THE YOUNG, 1836
ATTRIBUTED TO DOROTHY A. THRUPP

TAKE-AWAY THOUGHT

What key thought, phrase, or verse from this psalm
will you take with you into your day?

[1] Lawrence O. Richards, *The Bible Reader's Companion* (USA: Victor Books, 1991), quoted in QuickVerse 6.0 (Omaha: Parsons Technology, 2000).

[2] Ibid.

[3] Henry, 600.

Psalm 27

Preparing Your Heart

Ask God to quiet your heart and to speak to you through His Word. Ask Him to shine the light of His truth into your life. In this quiet moment, surrender yourself to Him and commit to obey whatever He shows you. Begin your time of devotion with this prayer:

> *Open my eyes that I may see*
> *wonderful things in your law.*
> *Give me understanding, and I will keep your law*
> *and obey it with all my heart.*
> *Show me your ways, O Lord,*
> *teach me your paths;*
> *guide me in your truth and teach me,*
> *for you are God my Savior,*
> *and my hope is in you all day long.*
> *Teach me what I cannot see;*
> *if I have done wrong, I will not do so again.*
>
> PSALM 119:18, 34; 25:4–5; JOB 34:32 NIV

$\mathscr{L}$istening to God

↷ Read Psalm 27 thoughtfully and prayerfully.

↷ What key words stand out to you in this passage?

↷ Write out a key verse from this passage.

↷ Summarize the entire passage in a sentence or two.

WHAT DOES THIS PASSAGE SAY?
(Observation)

1. What three things does David say that the Lord is to him (v. 1)?

2. How did David's relationship with God affect his response to opposition and attacks from the wicked (vv. 1–2)?

3. What was the number one desire and priority of David's life (v. 4)?

4. What statements express his dependence on God and his confidence in God?

_____

_____

5. List several of the petitions David makes of God in verses 7–12.

_____

_____

WHAT DOES THIS PASSAGE MEAN?
(Interpretation)

1. What needs in our lives are addressed by who God is—our light, our salvation, and the strength of our life (v. 1)?

_____

_____

2. Commenting on verse 4, John MacArthur notes, "The primary issue in David's life was to live in God's presence and by His purpose."[1] What does it mean to live in God's presence?

_____

_____

3. What is the significance of seeking God's face (vv. 8–9)?

_____

_____

"God's 'face' indicates His personal presence or simply His being; and seeking His face is a primary characteristic of true believers who desire fellowship with God."[2]

JOHN MACARTHUR

4. What is the connection between faith and waiting on the Lord (vv. 13–14)?

"Those who walk by faith in the goodness of the Lord shall in due time walk in the sight of that goodness."[3]

MATTHEW HENRY

HOW CAN I MAKE THIS PASSAGE A PART OF MY LIFE?
(Application)

1. In what circumstances might you be tempted to fear or to worry today? What does this passage reveal about God that can help strengthen your heart?

---

2. David was a man of singular focus, a man who steadfastly determined to seek the face and presence of God above all other goals (vv. 4, 8). What hindrances or distractions keep you from seeking God with all your heart?

---

3. What can you do to seek the face of God?

---

4. What is one area of your life where you need to wait on the Lord?

_____

_____

FOR FURTHER MEDITATION

Philippians 3:10–14

$\mathscr{R}$esponding to God

PRAISE

Praise God for what this passage reveals about His character, His heart, and His ways.

PRAYER

Confession: Tell God your need for His mercy. Confess any tendency you have had to lose heart or to be fearful in the midst of your circumstances.

Supplication: Ask the Lord to show you His face and teach you His ways. Ask Him to help you passionately pursue Him above all else.

Intercession: Use this passage as a basis to pray for someone whom God places on your heart.

SING TO THE LORD

Higher Ground

I'm pressing on the upward way,
New heights I'm gaining every day;
Still praying as I'm onward bound,
"Lord, plant my feet on higher ground."

My heart has no desire to stay
Where doubts arise and fears dismay;
Tho' some may dwell where these abound,
My prayer, my aim, is higher ground.

I want to scale the utmost height
And catch a gleam of glory bright;
But still I'll pray till heav'n I've found,
"Lord, lead me on to higher ground."

Lord, lift me up and let me stand
By faith on heaven's tableland;
A higher plane than I have found—
Lord, plant my feet on higher ground.

JOHNSON OATMAN, JR.

TAKE-AWAY THOUGHT

What key thought, phrase, or verse from this psalm
will you take with you into your day?

---

[1] *MacArthur Study Bible,* 765.

[2] Ibid.

[3] Henry, 605.

Psalm 46

*P*reparing Your Heart

Ask God to quiet your heart and to speak to you through His Word. Ask Him to shine the light of His truth into your life. In this quiet moment, surrender yourself to Him and commit to obey whatever He shows you. Begin your time of devotion with this prayer:

> *Open my eyes that I may see*
> *wonderful things in your law.*
> *Give me understanding, and I will keep your law*
> *and obey it with all my heart.*
> *Show me your ways, O Lord,*
> *teach me your paths;*
> *guide me in your truth and teach me,*
> *for you are God my Savior,*
> *and my hope is in you all day long.*
> *Teach me what I cannot see;*
> *if I have done wrong, I will not do so again.*
>
> PSALM 119:18, 34; 25:4–5; JOB 34:32 NIV

$\mathscr{L}$istening to God

∞ Read Psalm 46 thoughtfully and prayerfully.

∞ What key words stand out to you in this passage?

∞ Write out a key verse from this passage.

∞ Summarize the entire passage in a sentence or two.

WHAT DOES THIS PASSAGE SAY?
(Observation)

1. The psalmist describes a number of devastating circumstances. What are they (vv. 2–3, 6, 9)?

2. Where does the psalmist turn in the midst of trouble? What does he find in the Lord (v. 1)?

3. Write out the psalmist's refrain (vv. 7, 11).

4. How do the waters of verses 2–3 compare with the waters of verse 4? How is God like a "river" in the midst of His people?

_____

_____

Did You Know?

Psalm 46 is the text that inspired Martin Luther's great hymn, "A Mighty Fortress Is Our God."

WHAT DOES THIS PASSAGE MEAN?
(Interpretation)

1. "The LORD of hosts is with us; the God of Jacob is our refuge" (v. 7). What difference should that make when everything around us seems to be shaken or in conflict?

_____

_____

2. What kinds of situations in our lives could be compared to earthquakes, floods, and wars?

_____

_____

3. When everything around you seems to be "falling apart," how can you find peace and stability? How can your heart be at rest in the midst of troubled circumstances?

_____

_____

"The enemies of the church may toss her as waves, but they shall not split her as rocks. She may be dipped in water as a feather, but shall not sink therein as lead. He that is a well of water within her to keep her from fainting, will also prove a wall of fire about her to preserve her from falling. Tried she may be, but destroyed she cannot be. Her foundation is the Rock of Ages, and her defense the everlasting Arms."[1]

WILLIAM SECKER

4. Since God is with us in the midst of calamity, how should we respond differently than those who don't know God?

_____

_____

_____

HOW CAN I MAKE THIS PASSAGE A PART OF MY LIFE?
(Application)

1. What disastrous, unsettling circumstances have you faced in your life? How has God been a refuge and a help to you?

_____

_____

_____

2. What circumstances are you currently facing that are beyond your ability to manage or control?

_____

_____

_____

3. How can you deliberately take refuge in God when your situation is in turmoil?

_____

_____

FOR FURTHER MEDITATION
Philippians 4:4–7

*R*esponding to God

PRAISE

Read through this psalm and personalize your praise for each description of who God is and each promise He makes (e.g., "God, I praise You for being my refuge—a shelter from danger. You are my strength when I am weak. . . . ").

PRAYER

Confession: Confess your unbelief and fear to God. Seek His forgiveness for not trusting Him to help you.

Supplication: Humbly ask your Father, "I do believe; help me overcome my unbelief!" (Mark 9:24b, NIV). Lift your eyes up above your circumstances and ask for His help.

Intercession: Use this passage as a basis to pray for someone whom God places on your heart.

SING TO THE LORD

A Mighty Fortress Is Our God

A mighty fortress is our God,
 a bulwark never failing;
Our helper He amid the flood
 of mortal ills prevailing.
For still our ancient foe
 doth seek to work us woe—
His craft and pow'r are great,
And armed with cruel hate,
 on earth is not his equal.

Did we in our own strength confide,
 our striving would be losing;
Were not the right Man on our side,
 the Man of God's own choosing.
Dost ask who that may be?
 Christ Jesus, it is He;
Lord Sabaoth His name,
From age to age the same,
 and He must win the battle.

And tho' this world with devils filled,
 should threaten to undo us,
We will not fear for God has willed
 His truth to triumph through us.
The prince of darkness grim,
 we tremble not for him—
his rage we can endure,
for lo, his doom is sure;
 one little word shall fell him.

That word above all earthly pow'rs,
 no thanks to them, abideth;
The Spirit and the gifts are ours
 thro' Him who with us sideth.
Let goods and kindred go,
 this mortal life also—
the body they may kill;
God's truth abideth still:
 His kingdom is forever.

MARTIN LUTHER

TAKE-AWAY THOUGHT

*What key thought, phrase, or verse from this psalm
will you take with you into your day?*

---

[1] Spurgeon, *Treasury of David*, 220.

Psalm 57

♡ Preparing Your Heart

Ask God to quiet your heart and to speak to you through His Word. Ask Him to shine the light of His truth into your life. In this quiet moment, surrender yourself to Him and commit to obey whatever He shows you. Begin your time of devotion with this prayer:

> *Open my eyes that I may see*
> *   wonderful things in your law.*
> *Give me understanding, and I will keep your law*
> *   and obey it with all my heart.*
> *Show me your ways, O Lord,*
> *   teach me your paths;*
> *guide me in your truth and teach me,*
> *   for you are God my Savior,*
> *   and my hope is in you all day long.*
> *Teach me what I cannot see;*
> *   if I have done wrong, I will not do so again.*
>
> PSALM 119:18, 34; 25:4–5; JOB 34:32 NIV

$\mathcal{L}$istening to God

∞ Read Psalm 57 thoughtfully and prayerfully.

∞ What key words stand out to you in this passage?

∞ Write out a key verse from this passage.

∞ Summarize the entire passage in a sentence or two.

WHAT DOES THIS PASSAGE SAY?
(Observation)

1. According to the title of this psalm, where was David when he prayed this prayer? Why was he there?

_____

_____

To learn more of the background behind David's prayer, read 1 Samuel 22:1; 23:14–29; 24:1–22.

2. List three specific steps of action David took in the midst of his calamities:

(v. 1) _____

(v. 2) _____

(vv. 7, 9) _____

"Though David finds himself hiding from Saul, he knows that his real refuge is not in the walls of the cave, but in the shadow of God's wings."[1]

JOHN MACARTHUR

3. What was the condition of David's heart in the midst of being pursued (v. 7)?

_____

_____

4. What was David's supreme priority in the midst of the storms and trials he was facing (vv. 5, 11)?

_____

_____

WHAT DOES THIS PASSAGE MEAN?
(Interpretation)

1. What would be someone's natural reaction to David's circumstances?

_____

_____

2. How did David's response demonstrate faith?

_____

_____

3. What is the significance of knowing that God is "God Most High"? How should that reality affect our perspectives on our problems?

_____

_____

4. If our motivation is for God to be exalted and glorified, how does that affect our response to difficult circumstances?

5. How can our trouble and trials ultimately become a means of testimony to those who do not know God (vv. 9–10)?

HOW CAN I MAKE THIS PASSAGE A PART OF MY LIFE?
(Application)

1. What "storms" or attacks are you facing now?

2. How have you responded to your troubles?

3. Are you more concerned about getting relief from your problems or about God being magnified through your problems? How can you use your current circumstances to bring glory to God?

"A truly godly person wants God's glory to be exhibited more than he wants his own personal problems to be solved."[2]

JOHN MACARTHUR

4. What insights from this passage can help you keep a "steadfast" heart when you are in the midst of a storm?

_____

_____

FOR FURTHER MEDITATION

1 Peter 5:8–11

$\mathcal{R}$esponding to God

PRAISE

What does this passage teach you about the nature, heart, and ways of God? Praise Him for His protection, His purposes, and His promises.

PRAYER

Confession: Acknowledge any lack of faith that has been evident in your response to your circumstances.

Supplication: Ask God to glorify Himself through the circumstances of your life.

Intercession: Use this passage as a basis to pray for someone whom God places on your heart.

SING TO THE LORD

When Morning Gilds the Skies

When morning gilds the skies, my heart awaking cries:
May Jesus Christ be praised!
Alike at work or prayer, to Jesus I repair;
May Jesus Christ be praised!

Does sadness fill my mind, a solace here I find:
May Jesus Christ be praised!
Or fades my earthly bliss, my comfort still is this:
May Jesus Christ be praised!

In Heaven's eternal bliss, the loveliest strain is this,
May Jesus Christ be praised!
The powers of darkness fear, when this sweet chant they hear:
May Jesus Christ be praised!

Be this, while life is mine, my canticle divine:
May Jesus Christ be praised!
Be this th'eternal song through all the ages long:
May Jesus Christ be praised!

KATHOLISCHES GESANGBUCH, WURZBURG, 1828

TRANSLATED BY EDWARD CASWALL

TAKE-AWAY THOUGHT

What key thought, phrase, or verse from this psalm
will you take with you into your day?

---

[1] *MacArthur Study Bible*, 792–793.

[2] Ibid, 793.

Preparing Your Heart

Ask God to quiet your heart and to speak to you through His Word. Ask Him to shine the light of His truth into your life. In this quiet moment, surrender yourself to Him and commit to obey whatever He shows you. Begin your time of devotion with this prayer:

> *Open my eyes that I may see*
> *wonderful things in your law.*
> *Give me understanding, and I will keep your law*
> *and obey it with all my heart.*
> *Show me your ways, O Lord,*
> *teach me your paths;*
> *guide me in your truth and teach me,*
> *for you are God my Savior,*
> *and my hope is in you all day long.*
> *Teach me what I cannot see;*
> *if I have done wrong, I will not do so again.*
>
> PSALM 119:18, 34; 25:4–5; JOB 34:32 NIV

$\mathcal{L}$istening to God

❧ Read Psalm 71 thoughtfully and prayerfully.

❧ What key words stand out to you in this passage?

❧ Write out a key verse from this passage.

❧ Summarize the entire passage in a sentence or two.

WHAT DOES THIS PASSAGE SAY?
(Observation)

1. In what season of life does it appear the psalmist was when he wrote this psalm (vv. 5–6, 9, 17–18)?

2. As he looks back over his life, what things stand out to him? What has he learned about God?

3. What are some of the problems the psalmist faces as an older man (vv. 4, 9–13)?

4. Many of the psalms have a turning point, where despair turns to hope and prayer turns to praise. What verse is the turning point in Psalm 71?

_____

_____

5. Which verses in this psalm refer to the tongue, mouth, or lips? Instead of publicly defending his reputation when maligned, what does the psalmist talk about?

_____

_____

6. According to verses 3, 6, and 14, what does the psalmist do continually?

_____

_____

WHAT DOES THIS PASSAGE MEAN?
(Interpretation)

1. How does a long history of walking with God and experiencing His faithfulness help the psalmist deal with the unique challenges he faces as an older man?

_____

_____

2. What does this passage suggest about the importance and value of knowing and walking with God during childhood and youth?

_____

_____

> *"Those that have been taught of God from their youth, and have made it the business of their lives to honour him, may be sure that he will not leave them when they are old and grey-headed, but will make the evil days of old age their best days."* [1]
>
> MATTHEW HENRY

3. When we come to the season of life when our physical strength fails, how can we find strength to go on (vv. 9, 16)?

4. Why is it important for older believers to tell the next generation what they have learned about the heart and ways of God?

> *"It is a debt which the old disciples of Christ owe to the succeeding generations to leave behind them a solemn testimony to the power, pleasure, and advantage of religion, and the truth of God's promises."* [2]
>
> MATTHEW HENRY

HOW CAN I MAKE THIS PASSAGE A PART OF MY LIFE?
(Application)

1. What fears do you have about growing older?

2. What insights in this psalm can help you face your declining years with hope?

3. What impact will the choices you are making now have when you are older?

_____

_____

"I frequently hear persons in old age say how they would live, if they were to live their lives over again: Resolved, That I will live just so as I can think I shall wish I had done, supposing I live to old age."[3]

JONATHAN EDWARDS (WRITTEN AT AGE 19)

4. What lessons have you learned about the heart and ways of God from older believers?

_____

_____

5. What are some practical ways you can begin influencing younger believers to know and walk with God?

_____

_____

FOR FURTHER MEDITATION

2 Timothy 4:6b–8; 2 Peter 1:10–15

$\mathcal{R}$esponding to God

PRAISE

Join the psalmist in praising God for His righteousness (vv. 2, 15, 19, 24), His salvation (v. 15), His wondrous works (v. 17), His strength (v. 18), His power (v. 18), and His faithfulness (v. 22).

PRAYER

↪ *Confession:* Release any fears about the future that you may have allowed to control your thinking.

↪ *Supplication:* Ask God to help you glorify Him in your older years and to help you make Him known to those who come behind.

↪ *Intercession:* Pray for one or more elderly saints whom God puts on your heart. Pray that they will find a refuge in Him and that they will be faithful to make Him known—all the way to the finish line.

SING TO THE LORD

Great Is Thy Faithfulness

Great is Thy faithfulness, O God, my Father;
There is no shadow of turning with Thee.
Thou changest not; Thy compassions, they fail not.
As Thou has been Thou forever wilt be.

Summer and winter, and springtime and harvest,
Sun, moon, and stars in their courses above,
Join with all nature in manifold witness
To Thy great faithfulness, mercy and love.

Pardon for sin and a peace that endureth,
Thy own dear presence to cheer and to guide.
Strength for today and bright hope for tomorrow—
Blessings all mine with ten thousand beside!

Great is Thy faithfulness! Great is Thy faithfulness!
Morning by morning new mercies I see;
All I have needed Thy hand hath provided.
Great is Thy faithfulness, Lord, unto me!

THOMAS O. CHISHOLM

TAKE-AWAY THOUGHT

What key thought, phrase, or verse from this psalm
will you take with you into your day?

[1] Henry, 653.

[2] Ibid.

[3] *The Works of Jonathan Edwards*, vol. 1, Edward Hickman, ed., Sereno E. Dwight, memoir (Edinburgh: The Banner of Truth Trust, 1976), xxii.

Psalm 91

Preparing Your Heart

Ask God to quiet your heart and to speak to you through His Word. Ask Him to shine the light of His truth into your life. In this quiet moment, surrender yourself to Him and commit to obey whatever He shows you. Begin your time of devotion with this prayer:

> *Open my eyes that I may see*
> *wonderful things in your law.*
> *Give me understanding, and I will keep your law*
> *and obey it with all my heart.*
> *Show me your ways, O Lord,*
> *teach me your paths;*
> *guide me in your truth and teach me,*
> *for you are God my Savior,*
> *and my hope is in you all day long.*
> *Teach me what I cannot see;*
> *if I have done wrong, I will not do so again.*
>
> PSALM 119:18, 34; 25:4–5; JOB 34:32 NIV

*L*istening to God

- Read Psalm 91 thoughtfully and prayerfully.
- What key words stand out to you in this passage?

- Write out a key verse from this passage.

- Summarize the entire passage in a sentence or two.

WHAT DOES THIS PASSAGE SAY?
(Observation)

1. What four names of God are found in verses 1–2? What do they tell you about God?

_____

_____

2. What kinds of dangers does the psalmist identify in this psalm (vv. 3, 5–6, 10, 12–13)?

_____

_____

3. Where does the psalmist find shelter from danger (vv. 1–2, 4, 9)?

_____

_____

FOR FURTHER INSIGHT

"In a land where the sun can be oppressive and dangerous, a 'shadow' was understood as a metaphor for care and protection." [1]

JOHN MACARTHUR

4. What means does God provide for the believer's protection (vv. 4, 11)?

_____

_____

5. What blessings does God promise for those who trust Him and take refuge in Him?

_____

_____

"The blessings here promised are not for all believers but for those who live in close fellowship with God." [2]

CHARLES H. SPURGEON

WHAT DOES THIS PASSAGE MEAN?
(Interpretation)

1. How can believers experience safety, security, and serenity in the midst of spiritual danger and attack?

_____

_____

"To men who dwell in God, the most evil forces become harmless. . . . Their feet come into contact with the worst of foes. Even Satan himself nibbles at their heel, but in Christ Jesus they have the assured hope of bruising Satan under their feet shortly." [3]

CHARLES H. SPURGEON

2. What phrases do verses 3–6 and 13 use to describe the attacks of Satan on the people of God?

_____

_____

3. Does this passage teach that God's people will be exempt from danger, pressures, and problems? What light does the Apostle Paul shed on this question in 2 Corinthians 11:23–28 and 12:7–10?

_____

_____

4. What conditions must we meet in order to experience God's protection from danger and attack (vv. 1, 2, 4, 9, 14, 15)?

_____

_____

HOW CAN I MAKE THIS PASSAGE A PART OF MY LIFE?
(Application)

1. Where do most people turn for refuge in the midst of trouble?

_____

_____

2. Where do you tend to turn for refuge?

_____

_____

3. What spiritual dangers or enemies are you encountering at this time or have you encountered recently?

_____

_____

4. How can you deliberately take refuge in God?

_____

_____

FOR FURTHER MEDITATION

Psalm 142:3b–5; Ephesians 6:10–13

$\mathscr{R}$esponding to God

PRAISE

What does this passage reveal to you about God and His ways? Praise Him for His protection and His promises.

PRAYER

Confession: Have you been responding to any of your circumstances with fear, anxiety, or worry? Confess those times when you have failed to trust fully in Him.

Supplication: Express to God your desire to take refuge in Him, to live under the shadow and protection of His wings, and to walk by faith, even in the midst of trouble.

Intercession: Use this passage as a basis to pray for someone whom God places on your heart.

SING TO THE LORD

Under His Wings

Under His wings I am safely abiding.
Tho' the night deepens and tempests are wild,
Still I can trust Him; I know He will keep me.
He has redeemed me, and I am His child.

  Under His wings, under His wings,
  Who from His love can sever?
  Under His wings my soul shall abide,
  Safely abide forever.

Under His wings—what a refuge in sorrow!
How the heart yearningly turns to His rest!
Often when earth has no balm for my healing,
There I find comfort, and there I am blest.

Under His wings—O what precious enjoyment!
There will I hide till life's trials are o'er;
Sheltered, protected, no evil can harm me.
Resting in Jesus, I'm safe evermore.

WILLIAM O. CUSHING

TAKE-AWAY THOUGHT

*What key thought, phrase, or verse from this psalm
will you take with you into your day?*

---

[1] *MacArthur Study Bible,* 824.

[2] Spurgeon, *Treasury of David,* 383.

[3] Ibid., 387.

*P*reparing Your Heart

Ask God to quiet your heart and to speak to you through His Word. Ask Him to shine the light of His truth into your life. In this quiet moment, surrender yourself to Him and commit to obey whatever He shows you. Begin your time of devotion with this prayer:

> *Open my eyes that I may see*
> *wonderful things in your law.*
> *Give me understanding, and I will keep your law*
> *and obey it with all my heart.*
> *Show me your ways, O Lord,*
> *teach me your paths;*
> *guide me in your truth and teach me,*
> *for you are God my Savior,*
> *and my hope is in you all day long.*
> *Teach me what I cannot see;*
> *if I have done wrong, I will not do so again.*
>
> PSALM 119:18, 34; 25:4–5; JOB 34:32 NIV

$\mathcal{L}$istening to God

- Read Psalm 121 thoughtfully and prayerfully.

- What key words stand out to you in this passage?

- Write out a key verse from this passage.

- Summarize the entire passage in a sentence or two.

WHAT DOES THIS PASSAGE SAY?
(Observation)

Getting the Setting

Psalms 120—134 are "Songs of Ascents," which Jewish pilgrims sang on their way up to Jerusalem (about 2700 feet in elevation) on the occasions of three annual feasts.

1. What words does this psalm use to describe God's relationship to and His care for His people?

2. Circle each time the words *keeper, keep, preserve, watch,* or *watches* appear in this psalm. These are all translated from the same Hebrew word that means "to keep, guard, preserve, protect, watch (as a watchman of sheep or cattle), to hedge about something (as with thorns)."[1]

3. What phrase describes the immensity and power of God (v. 2)?

4. What image shows the nearness of God and the intimacy we may experience with Him (v. 5)?

5. What are some of the things that God protects and preserves His people from?

6. Human caretakers have limitations—they cannot be on duty around the clock; their services are not available forever; they cannot protect from every kind of danger; they cannot protect the innermost parts of our heart. By comparison, what words or phrases in this psalm describe the *limitless extent* of God's protective care over His people?

WHAT DOES THIS PASSAGE MEAN?
(Interpretation)

1. What are some of the sources people look to for help and protection?

2. What are the implications of the fact that God is the Creator of heaven and earth?

3. What benefits do we receive from shade? How is God like shade to His people?

4. What attitudes or behaviors suggest that a person is not trusting God as his Keeper?

5. What attitudes or behaviors indicate that a person *is* trusting God as his Keeper?

"It is vain to trust the creatures: it is wise to trust the Creator. . . . None are so safe as those whom God keeps; none so much in danger as the self-secure."[2]

CHARLES H. SPURGEON

HOW CAN I MAKE THIS PASSAGE A PART OF MY LIFE?
(Application)

1. What kind of help do you need in your life at this time?

_____

_____

2. To what or to whom have you been looking for help?

_____

_____

3. What are some practical steps you can take to completely transfer your trust from fallible sources to God alone?

_____

_____

4. This passage describes God's constant, watchful care over His people. Write a short response to God, expressing your trust in Him as your Keeper.

_____

_____

FOR FURTHER MEDITATION
John 17:11–12, 15; 1 Thessalonians 5:23; Jude 24–25

Responding to God

PRAISE

Praise God for specific instances when He has protected you from evil or danger. Praise Him for His promise to preserve your soul for all time and eternity.

PRAYER

Confession: Admit your tendencies toward relying on yourself, other people, or other things to help you, rather than on God.

Supplication: Based on this psalm, ask God to guard your heart and your footsteps this day.

Intercession: Use this passage as a basis to pray for someone whom God places on your heart.

SING TO THE LORD

Children of the Heavenly Father

Children of the heav'nly Father safely in His bosom gather;
Nestling bird nor star in heaven such a refuge e'er was given.

God His own doth tend and nourish; in His holy courts they flourish.
From all evil things He spares them; in His mighty arms He bears them.

Neither life nor death shall ever from the Lord His children sever;
Unto them His grace He showeth, and their sorrows all He knoweth.

Tho' He giveth or He taketh, God His children ne'er forsaketh;
His the loving purpose solely to preserve them pure and holy.

CAROLINA SANDELL BERG
TRANSLATED BY ERNST W. OLSON

TAKE-AWAY THOUGHT

What key thought, phrase, or verse from this psalm
will you take with you into your day?

[1] *Word Study Old Testament,* 2376.
[2] Spurgeon, *Treasury of David,* 573, 575.

*P*salm 25

♡ *P*reparing Your Heart

Ask God to quiet your heart and to speak to you through His Word. Ask Him to shine the light of His truth into your life. In this quiet moment, surrender yourself to Him and commit to obey whatever He shows you. Begin your time of devotion with this prayer:

> *Open my eyes that I may see*
>   *wonderful things in your law.*
> *Give me understanding, and I will keep your law*
>   *and obey it with all my heart.*
> *Show me your ways, O Lord,*
>   *teach me your paths;*
> *guide me in your truth and teach me,*
>   *for you are God my Savior,*
>   *and my hope is in you all day long.*
> *Teach me what I cannot see;*
>   *if I have done wrong, I will not do so again.*
>
>   PSALM 119:18, 34; 25:4–5; JOB 34:32 NIV

*L*istening to God

- Read Psalm 25 thoughtfully and prayerfully.
- What key words stand out to you in this passage?

- Write out a key verse from this passage.

- Summarize the entire passage in a sentence or two.

WHAT DOES THIS PASSAGE SAY?
(Observation)

Did You Know?

This psalm is an acrostic. With two exceptions, every verse begins with a successive letter of the Hebrew alphabet. Psalms 9, 10, 34, 37, 111, 112, 119, and 145 are also structured as acrostics.

1. How does David describe his circumstances and the emotional state that motivated this prayer (vv. 16–18)?

2. What are the two major causes of David's anguish (vv. 2, 19; vv. 7, 11, 18)?

"It is the mark of a true saint that his sorrows remind him of his sins, and his sorrow for sin drives him to his God."[1]

CHARLES H. SPURGEON

3. What is David's response in the midst of His distress?

(v. 1)

(vv. 4–5)

(vv. 7, 11)

(v. 15)

(v. 20)

4. On what basis does he ask God to forgive his sins (vv. 6, 7, 11)?

"'Forgive all my sins' is the cry of a soul that is more sick of sin than of pain and would sooner be forgiven than healed. Blessed is the man to whom sin is more unbearable than disease; he shall not be long before the Lord shall both forgive his iniquity and heal his diseases. Men are slow to see the intimate connection between sin and sorrow."[2]

CHARLES H. SPURGEON

"He is moved to mercy towards us by nothing in us but the miserableness of our case. It is the honor of Christ to save the greatest sinners when they come to Him, as it is the honor of a physician that he cures the most desperate diseases or wounds."[3]

JONATHAN EDWARDS

5. What kind of person does God teach and guide (vv. 8, 9, 12)?

6. How does David evidence a humble heart in this passage?

WHAT DOES THIS PASSAGE MEAN?
(Interpretation)

1. How does the fear of the Lord result in greater intimacy with God (v. 12)?

_____

_____

> *"Walking with God is the best way to know the mind of God; friends who walk together impart their secrets one to another."*[4]
>
> THOMAS WATSON

2. What lessons can you learn from David's response to affliction?

_____

_____

3. Why is it important to be conscious of any connection between your sin and your difficult life circumstances? How does having a humble heart help you make the connection?

_____

_____

HOW CAN I MAKE THIS PASSAGE A PART OF MY LIFE?
(Application)

1. Are you more concerned about your sin against God than about getting relief from the pressures and problems in your life? (See v. 18.)

_____

_____

_____

"Pharaoh more lamented the hard strokes that were upon him than the hard heart which was within him. Esau mourned not because he sold the birthright, which was his sin, but because he lost the blessing, which was his punishment. . . . Many complain more of the sorrows to which they are born than of the sins with which they were born."[5]

WILLIAM SECKER

2. Do you take your sin as seriously as David took his? How can you cultivate greater sensitivity to sin and a greater sense of how sin pains God?

_____

_____

3. God reveals His ways to the humble. How humble and teachable is your heart? Would other people describe you as having a teachable or a stubborn spirit?

_____

_____

4. "The secret [the counsel, friendship, intimacy] of the Lord is with those who fear Him" (v. 14). To fear the Lord is to have a reverential awe for Him and to share His hatred of sin. How can you develop a greater sense of the fear of the Lord?

_____

_____

FOR FURTHER MEDITATION

James 4:8–10

*R*esponding to God

PRAISE

Praise God for not remembering the sins of your youth but for remembering you according to His mercy and His lovingkindness in Christ (vv. 6–7).

PRAYER

- Pray through this psalm and personalize the requests. Make the cry of David's heart the cry of your own heart.

- Select one or more verses in this passage to pray for someone whom God puts on your heart.

SING TO THE LORD

I Am Trusting Thee, Lord Jesus

I am trusting Thee, Lord Jesus—trusting only Thee;
Trusting Thee for full salvation, great and free.

I am trusting Thee to guide me—Thou alone shalt lead,
Every day and hour supplying all my need.

I am trusting Thee for power—Thine can never fail;
Words which Thou Thyself shalt give me must prevail.

I am trusting Thee, Lord Jesus—never let me fall;
I am trusting Thee forever, and for all.

FRANCES RIDLEY HAVERGAL

TAKE-AWAY THOUGHT

What key thought, phrase, or verse from this psalm
will you take with you into your day?

[1] Spurgeon, *Treasury of David*, 122.

[2] Ibid., 130.

[3] Ibid., 127.

[4] Ibid., 129.

[5] Ibid., 128.

Preparing Your Heart

Ask God to quiet your heart and to speak to you through His Word. Ask Him to shine the light of His truth into your life. In this quiet moment, surrender yourself to Him and commit to obey whatever He shows you. Begin your time of devotion with this prayer:

> *Open my eyes that I may see*
> *wonderful things in your law.*
> *Give me understanding, and I will keep your law*
> *and obey it with all my heart.*
> *Show me your ways, O Lord,*
> *teach me your paths;*
> *guide me in your truth and teach me,*
> *for you are God my Savior,*
> *and my hope is in you all day long.*
> *Teach me what I cannot see;*
> *if I have done wrong, I will not do so again.*
>
> PSALM 119:18, 34; 25:4–5; JOB 34:32 NIV

ℒistening to God

- Read Psalm 42 thoughtfully and prayerfully.

- What key words stand out to you in this passage?

- Write out a key verse from this passage.

- Summarize the entire passage in a sentence or two.

WHAT DOES THIS PASSAGE SAY?
(Observation)

"The Sons of Korah"

A total of eleven psalms are associated with this group of Levites (mentioned in Num 26:10ff; 1 Chron 6:22ff; 2 Chron 20:19). The heading probably indicates that these psalms were given to them to be performed, not that they actually penned the psalms—meaning, for the sons of Korah.

Getting the Setting

The psalmist (probably David) is far removed from the place (Jerusalem) where he has long loved to worship God. He now lives in the northern part of Palestine (v. 6) and is unable to make the pilgrimage to the house of the Lord. His enemies do not share his longing for God and constantly taunt him. The psalmist is despondent and plagued with questions and doubts as a result of his tumultuous circumstances and the apparent absence of God.

Note: Psalms 42 and 43 were probably originally one psalm. Reading the psalms together provides further insight into the psalmist's struggle to sustain an intimate relationship with God when he had no visible means of support for his faith.

1. What two images does the psalmist use to express the desperation he feels (vv. 1–2, vv. 7–8)?

_____

_____

2. Trace the conflict between *faith* (spiritual realities) and *sight* (human emotions and life circumstances) throughout this psalm:

(vv. 1–2) *Faith* says: _____

(vv. 3–4) *Sight* says: _____

(v. 5) *Faith* says: _____

(vv. 6–7) *Sight* says: _____

(v. 8) *Faith* says: _____

(vv. 9–10) *Sight* says: _____

(v. 11) *Faith* says: _____

WHAT DOES THIS PASSAGE MEAN?
(Interpretation)

The psalmist wrestles with despondency and depression caused by a sense of isolation from God, by the absence of fellowship and encouragement from godly friends, and by the relentless darts thrown at him by unbelievers. How does he deal with his tumultuous emotions?

He speaks to God.

1. What does he say to God (vv. 1–3, 6–7, 9)? What questions does he ask?

_____

_____

2. Why is it important for us to be honest with God about our doubts and struggles?

_____

_____

He speaks to himself.

3. What does he tell his heart (vv. 5, 11; 43:5)?

_____

_____

4. Why is it important for us to counsel our hearts with the truth? Why is it important for us to *keep* counseling our hearts with the same truth (vv. 5, 11, 43:5)?

_____

_____

> "We must talk to ourselves instead of allowing 'ourselves' to talk to us! . . . You must say to your soul: 'Why art thou cast down'—what business have you to be disquieted? You must . . . exhort yourself, and say to yourself: 'Hope thou in God'—instead of muttering in this depressed, unhappy way. And then you must go on to remind yourself of God, Who God is, and what God is, and what God has done, and what God has pledged Himself to do. Then having done that, end on this great note: defy yourself, and defy other people, and defy the devil and the whole world, and say with this man: 'I shall yet praise Him for the help of His countenance, who is also the health of my countenance and my God.'"[1]
>
> MARTYN LLOYD-JONES

HOW CAN I MAKE THIS PASSAGE A PART OF MY LIFE?
(Application)

1. Why might God sometimes allow us to be isolated from Christian fellowship and encouragement?

_____

_____

2. When have you wrestled with the emotions expressed in this psalm, when your soul was "cast down" and "disquieted" within you?

_____

_____

3. What does this passage reveal about the character and the ways of God that can help you walk by faith when you are downcast or depressed (vv. 2, 5, 8, 9, 11)?

_____

_____

4. What challenges are you facing at this time? Counsel your own heart, as David did, by writing out some meaningful truths about God and His ways.

_____

_____

FOR FURTHER MEDITATION

2 Corinthians 4:8–10, 16–18

$\mathscr{R}$esponding to God

PRAISE

Praise God for the reality of His presence, His promises, His protection, and His provision, regardless of how forsaken or downcast you may feel.

PRAYER

⊙ *Confession:* Honestly tell the Lord any doubts or fears you may be experiencing.

⊙ *Supplication:* Ask the Lord to help you to walk by faith, regardless of your emotions or your circumstances.

⊙ *Intercession:* Use this passage as a basis to pray for someone whom God places on your heart.

SING TO THE LORD

What a Friend We Have in Jesus

What a friend we have in Jesus, all our sins and griefs to bear!
What a privilege to carry everything to God in prayer!
O what peace we often forfeit, O what needless pain we bear,
All because we do not carry everything to God in prayer!

Have we trials and temptations? Is there trouble anywhere?
We should never be discouraged; take it to the Lord in prayer.
Can we find a friend so faithful who will all our sorrows share?
Jesus knows our every weakness; take it to the Lord in prayer.

Are we weak and heavy-laden, cumbered with a load of care?
Precious Savior, still our Refuge; take it to the Lord in prayer.
Do thy friends despise, forsake Thee? Take it to the Lord in prayer.
In His arms He'll take and shield thee; Thou wilt find a solace there.

JOSEPH M. SCRIVEN

TAKE-AWAY THOUGHT

What key thought, phrase, or verse from this psalm
will you take with you into your day?

---

[1] D. Martyn Lloyd-Jones, *Spiritual Depression: Its Causes and Cure* (Grand Rapids: Wm. B. Eerdmans Publishing Company, 1986), 20–21.

Psalm 85

Preparing Your Heart

Ask God to quiet your heart and to speak to you through His Word. Ask Him to shine the light of His truth into your life. In this quiet moment, surrender yourself to Him and commit to obey whatever He shows you. Begin your time of devotion with this prayer:

*Open my eyes that I may see
 wonderful things in your law.
Give me understanding, and I will keep your law
 and obey it with all my heart.
Show me your ways, O Lord,
 teach me your paths;
guide me in your truth and teach me,
 for you are God my Savior,
 and my hope is in you all day long.
Teach me what I cannot see;
 if I have done wrong, I will not do so again.*

PSALM 119:18, 34; 25:4–5; JOB 34:32 NIV

$\mathcal{L}$istening to God

- Read Psalm 85 thoughtfully and prayerfully.

- What key words stand out to you in this passage?

- Write out a key verse from this passage.

- Summarize the entire passage in a sentence or two.

WHAT DOES THIS PASSAGE SAY?
(Observation)

1. "Lord, You've done it before!" The psalmist recalls a time in the past when God revived His people. What were the marks of that season of blessing (vv. 1–3)?

2. "Lord, do it again!" The psalmist prays for a fresh work of revival in his day. What phrases indicate that revival is a sovereign work initiated by God (vv. 4–7)?

Spotlight on a Word

Revive: "to live anew; to recover; to be well; to make alive, enliven, animate, quicken; to refresh; to rebuild." [1]

3. What conditions must be met by God's people who long for revival (vv. 8, 9, 13)?

4. What are the anticipated fruits of revival (vv. 6, 8, 9, 12)?

"Joy is the very flavor of revival. We may have to go through deep humiliation to taste it, but rejoicing marks the church in revival."[2]

RAYMOND C. ORTLUND JR.

WHAT DOES THIS PASSAGE MEAN?
(Interpretation)

1. Circle every time the word "us" appears in verses 4–7. To whom is the psalmist referring when he prays, "Revive *us*" (vv. 6, 8)? When we pray for revival, whom are we asking God to revive?

2. Verses 3–5 include five references to God's anger. His anger is obviously an important theme of this psalm. What provokes God's anger? What causes His anger to cease?

"God's anger in verse 5 . . . is not a condemning anger, rejecting his people. It is a disciplining anger, refining his people. They are not living in such aggressive defiance of God that the psalmist calls for repentance. But God stands some distance away from his own people, because they have not been seeking him. They have been resting on the blessings of the past (vv. 1–3). They have drifted into spiritual complacency. And in fatherly discipline God is withholding the outpouring of new blessing until his children cry out to him in sharpened hunger."[3]

RAYMOND C. ORTLUND JR.

3. This passage reminds us that revival always points us back to Christ. Verse 10 says, "Mercy and truth have met together." How did Christ fulfill this picture? (See John 1:14.) What happens when mercy and truth meet together? (See Proverbs 16:6.)

4. "Righteousness and peace have kissed" (v. 10). How was this image fulfilled at the Cross?

5. How does verse 11 anticipate the Incarnation—the first coming of Christ to earth?

HOW CAN I MAKE THIS PASSAGE A PART OF MY LIFE?
(Application)

1. "I will hear what God the LORD will speak" (v. 8). What are some hindrances to hearing God speak?

_____

_____

2. What steps can you take to really listen to His voice every day?

_____

_____

3. "That glory may dwell in our land" (v. 9). If the glory of God (His manifest presence) were to dwell in our land, how would our culture be different? Our churches? Your family? Your life?

_____

_____

FOR FURTHER MEDITATION

Luke 1:68, 74–79

*R*esponding to God

PRAISE

Praise God for His reviving mercy. Praise Him for times in the past when He has revived the hearts and lives of His people. Praise Him that He is able to "do it again" in our day.

PRAYER

Confession: Examine your heart and admit any hindrances to revival that may be present in your life.

Supplication: Pray for a genuine revival in your life, in your family, in your church, in your nation, and throughout the world.

Intercession: Pray for the people of God, that He will grant us hearts that are humble and responsive toward Him.

SING TO THE LORD

Revive Us Again

We praise Thee, O God, for the Son of Thy love—
For Jesus, who died and is now gone above.

Hallelujah! Thine the glory! Hallelujah! Amen!
Hallelujah! Thine the glory! Revive us again.

We praise Thee, O God, for Thy Spirit of Light,
Who has shown us our Savior and scattered our night.

All glory and praise to the Lamb that was slain,
Who has borne all our sins and has cleansed every stain.

Revive us again; fill each heart with Thy love.
May each soul be rekindled with fire from above.

WILLIAM P. MACKAY

TAKE-AWAY THOUGHT

What key thought, phrase, or verse from this psalm
will you take with you into your day?

---

[1] *Word Study Old Testament*, 2315.

[2] Raymond C. Ortlund Jr., *When God Comes to Church* (Grand Rapids: Baker Books, 2000), 53.

[3] Ibid., 43.

Psalm 142

♡ *Preparing* Your Heart

Ask God to quiet your heart and to speak to you through His Word. Ask Him to shine the light of His truth into your life. In this quiet moment, surrender yourself to Him and commit to obey whatever He shows you. Begin your time of devotion with this prayer:

> *Open my eyes that I may see*
> *wonderful things in your law.*
> *Give me understanding, and I will keep your law*
> *and obey it with all my heart.*
> *Show me your ways, O Lord,*
> *teach me your paths;*
> *guide me in your truth and teach me,*
> *for you are God my Savior,*
> *and my hope is in you all day long.*
> *Teach me what I cannot see;*
> *if I have done wrong, I will not do so again.*
>
> PSALM 119:18, 34; 25:4–5; JOB 34:32 NIV

$\mathscr{L}$istening to God

- Read Psalm 142 thoughtfully and prayerfully.
- What key words stand out to you in this passage?

- Write out a key verse from this passage.

- Summarize the entire passage in a sentence or two.

WHAT DOES THIS PASSAGE SAY?
(Observation)

1. What words or phrases in this passage describe David's external circumstances? (See title, vv. 2–4, 6.)

_____

_____

2. What words describe his thoughts and feelings (vv. 3, 6)?

_____

_____

3. What was his response to his circumstances (vv. 1–2, 5)?

_____

_____

4. What was David's motive for asking God to deliver him (v. 7)?

_____

_____

5. This psalm is called a *maschil,* meaning a psalm of instruction or contemplation. What lessons did David learn when he was in the cave?

_____

_____

6. How did David express faith in the midst of his trial (v. 7)?

_____

_____

WHAT DOES THIS PASSAGE MEAN?
(Interpretation)

1. In what way was David's crisis really a blessing?

_____

_____

"Anything which leads us to cry unto God is a blessing to us." [1]

CHARLES H. SPURGEON

2. How did David get to know God better through his crisis?

_____

_____

3. What is the difference between pouring out your heart to the Lord and complaining about your circumstances to others? Why is one permissible and effective and the other not?

_____

_____

"We may complain to God, but not of God. When we complain, it should not be before men, but before God alone. . . . We do not show our trouble before the Lord that He may see it, but that we may see Him. It is for our relief, and not for His information that we make plain statements concerning our woes. . . . Pour out your thoughts, and you will see what they are: show your trouble, and the extent of it will be known to you: let all be done before the Lord, for in comparison with His great majesty of love the trouble will seem to be as nothing."[2]

CHARLES H. SPURGEON

HOW CAN I MAKE THIS PASSAGE A PART OF MY LIFE?
(Application)

4. Why is it encouraging to know that God knows the path you are walking (v. 3)?

_____

_____

5. How can times of loneliness benefit you?

_____

_____

6. What have you learned about God in the midst of your low points? How has God been a refuge to you in your times of trouble?

_____

_____

7. How can you help or encourage a friend who is in distress?

_____

_____

FOR FURTHER MEDITATION

Job 23:8–10; 2 Timothy 4:16–18

$\mathcal{R}$esponding to God

PRAISE

Praise God for what this passage reveals about His heart and His ways. Praise Him for the times He has been a refuge to you.

PRAYER

Confession: Admit any tendency you have to turn to people, rather than to God, to meet your needs.

Supplication: Pour out your heart to the Lord about any trouble you are facing. Be specific in telling Him your circumstances. Cry out to Him to be your refuge and your portion.

Intercession: Use this passage as a basis to pray for someone whom God places on your heart.

SING TO THE LORD

I Must Tell Jesus

I must tell Jesus all of my trials; I cannot bear these burdens alone.
In my distress He kindly will help me; He ever loves and cares for His own.

I must tell Jesus all of my troubles; He is a kind, compassionate Friend.
If I but ask Him, He will deliver, make of my troubles quickly an end.

O how the world to evil allures me! O how my heart is tempted to sin!
I must tell Jesus, and He will help me over the world the vict'ry to win.

I must tell Jesus! I must tell Jesus! I cannot bear my burdens alone;
I must tell Jesus! I must tell Jesus! Jesus can help me, Jesus alone.

ELISHA A. HOFFMAN

TAKE-AWAY THOUGHT

What key thought, phrase, or verse from this psalm
will you take with you into your day?

---

[1] Spurgeon, *Treasury of David*, 655.
[2] Ibid., 654.

Psalm 139

*P*reparing Your Heart

Ask God to quiet your heart and to speak to you through His Word. Ask Him to shine the light of His truth into your life. In this quiet moment, surrender yourself to Him and commit to obey whatever He shows you. Begin your time of devotion with this prayer:

> *Open my eyes that I may see*
> > *wonderful things in your law.*
> *Give me understanding, and I will keep your law*
> > *and obey it with all my heart.*
> *Show me your ways, O Lord,*
> > *teach me your paths;*
> *guide me in your truth and teach me,*
> > *for you are God my Savior,*
> > *and my hope is in you all day long.*
> *Teach me what I cannot see;*
> > *if I have done wrong, I will not do so again.*
>
> > PSALM 119:18, 34; 25:4–5; JOB 34:32 NIV

$\mathscr{L}$istening to God

- Read Psalm 139 thoughtfully and prayerfully.
- What key words stand out to you in this passage?

- Write out a key verse from this passage.

- Summarize the entire passage in a sentence or two.

WHAT DOES THIS PASSAGE SAY?
(Observation)

1. David was in awe of God. Which of God's attributes does he marvel at in each of the following sections (vv. 1–6; vv. 7–12; vv. 13–18)?

_____

_____

2. How did David feel about those who hate God (vv. 19–22)?

_____

_____

> *"To hate a man for his own sake, or for any evil done to us, would be wrong; but to hate a man because he is the foe of all goodness and the enemy of all righteousness, is nothing more nor less than an obligation. The more we love God, the more indignant shall we grow with those who refuse Him their affection."*[1]
>
> CHARLES H. SPURGEON

3. How do verses 23–24 reveal that David's heart attitude while he prayed against God's enemies was humble and sincere rather than arrogant and hypocritical?

WHAT DOES THIS PASSAGE MEAN?
(Interpretation)

1. David said that God had "hedged" or "hemmed" him in (v. 5). What does this tell you about the way God cares for His children?

---

2. What is the underlying message of this psalm? How does it address your daily problems—worry, fear, anxiety, etc.?

---

3. What broader perspective do we gain by knowing that our days on earth were numbered and planned before they began (v. 16)?

---

4. How did David's perspective on God's enemies differ from the philosophy of "tolerance" that is so prevalent in our day? What tolerance should we have for evil? How should we react to those who blaspheme God and practice evil as a lifestyle (vv. 19–22)?

---

5. Since David had already acknowledged that God knew everything about him, why then did he ask God to search him and know him (vv. 23–24)?

"Before men, we stand as opaque beehives. They can see the thoughts go in and out of us, but what work they do inside of a man they cannot tell. Before God we are as glass beehives, and all that our thoughts are doing within us He perfectly sees and understands."[2]

HENRY WARD BEECHER

HOW CAN I MAKE THIS PASSAGE A PART OF MY LIFE?
(Application)

1. Write a sentence of response to God for each of His incredible attributes described in this psalm. Express to Him what difference He makes in your life.

His omniscience—He knows everything about you, including your actions, words, and motives.

His omnipresence—God is with you in every place.

His creatorship—God designed and made every part of you.

His sovereignty—God knew all about you and ordered every one of your days before you were even conceived.

His attentiveness—God is always thinking about you; His loving thoughts toward you cannot be numbered.

---

2. Even though we understand that there is no physical place where we can hide from God, we still sometimes try to escape Him through activities, relationships, and other pursuits. In what ways do you try to hide from God? Why do you sometimes hold God at a distance?

_____

_____

3. Understanding that God knew all about us before we were even conceived can enable us to accept the way He made us. What things about yourself have you had difficulty accepting, perhaps even to the point of questioning God?

_____

_____

4. Are you tolerating evil in any form—wrong relationships, entertainment, habits, etc.? How can you respond differently?

_____

_____

FOR FURTHER MEDITATION

Hebrews 4:12–16

*R*esponding to God

PRAISE

Adore God for each of His attributes revealed in this psalm.

115

PRAYER

Confession: In the spirit of David's prayer, ask God to search your heart for any anxiety or any offensive way. Agree with Him about whatever He shows you.

Supplication: Ask the Lord to lead you in the way that is pleasing to Him and to give you a heart to trust and follow Him.

Intercession: Use this passage as a basis to pray for someone whom God places on your heart.

SING TO THE LORD

Search Me, O God

Search me, O God, and know my heart today;
Try me, O Savior, know my thoughts, I pray.
See if there be some wicked way in me;
Cleanse me from every sin and set me free.

I praise Thee, Lord, for cleansing me from sin;
Fulfill Thy Word and make me pure within.
Fill me with fire where once I burned with shame;
Grant my desire to magnify Thy name.

Lord, take my life and make it wholly Thine;
Fill my poor heart with Thy great love divine.
Take all my will, my passion, self and pride;
I now surrender, Lord—in me abide.

O Holy Ghost, revival comes from Thee;
Send a revival, start the work in me.
Thy Word declares Thou wilt supply our need;
For blessings now, O Lord, I humbly plead.

J. EDWIN ORR

TAKE-AWAY THOUGHT

What key thought, phrase, or verse from this psalm
will you take with you into your day?

[1] Spurgeon, *Treasury of David*, 642.
[2] Ibid., 635.

Psalm 32

♡ Preparing Your Heart

Ask God to quiet your heart and to speak to you through His Word. Ask Him to shine the light of His truth into your life. In this quiet moment, surrender yourself to Him and commit to obey whatever He shows you. Begin your time of devotion with this prayer:

> *Open my eyes that I may see*
> *wonderful things in your law.*
> *Give me understanding, and I will keep your law*
> *and obey it with all my heart.*
> *Show me your ways, O Lord,*
> *teach me your paths;*
> *guide me in your truth and teach me,*
> *for you are God my Savior,*
> *and my hope is in you all day long.*
> *Teach me what I cannot see;*
> *if I have done wrong, I will not do so again.*
>
> PSALM 119:18, 34; 25:4–5; JOB 34:32 NIV

✑istening to God

- Read Psalm 32 thoughtfully and prayerfully.

- What key words stand out to you in this passage?

- Write out a key verse from this passage.

- Summarize the entire passage in a sentence or two.

WHAT DOES THIS PASSAGE SAY?
(Observation)

1. What words does David use to speak of his offenses against God (vv. 1–2)?

2. Describe the consequences David experienced when he tried to cover his sin and refused to acknowledge it before God (vv. 3–4).

3. How did David find relief from the burden of his guilt (v. 5)?

> *"The word rendered forgiven is, in the original, 'taken off,' or 'taken away,' as a burden is lifted or a barrier removed. What a lift is here! It cost our Savior a sweat of blood to bear our load, yea, it cost Him His life to bear it quite away."*[1]

CHARLES H. SPURGEON

4. Based on his personal experience (vv. 1–5), what instruction did David offer to others who want to experience the same blessedness he experienced (vv. 6–11)?

> *"Thou art my hiding place. Observe that the same man who in the fourth verse was oppressed by the presence of God here finds a shelter in Him. See what honest confession and full forgiveness will do! The gospel of substitution makes Him to be our refuge who otherwise would have been our Judge."*[2]

CHARLES H. SPURGEON

WHAT DOES THIS PASSAGE MEAN?
(Interpretation)

1. In what sense is the repentance that David describes a one-time experience that occurs at salvation as well as an ongoing need in the life of every believer?

---

2. Why is it important not to delay confessing our sin to the Lord (v. 6)?

---

3. What blessings and benefits are experienced by those who confess and repent of their sins (vv. 1–2, 5, 7, 10–11)?

4. What do the images of the horse and the mule mean (v. 9)? What lesson are we encouraged to learn from them?

HOW CAN I MAKE THIS PASSAGE A PART OF MY LIFE?
(Application)

1. Describe a time when you experienced the blessedness of confessing your sin and being assured of His forgiveness.

2. Describe a time when you kept silent about your sin and tried to cover it.

3. Have you ever experienced the type of intense conviction over your sin that David describes in verses 3–4? Describe what that experience felt like.

4. What sin do you need to acknowledge to the Lord?

_____

_____

FOR FURTHER MEDITATION
Proverbs 28:13; 1 John 1:8–10

ℛesponding to God

PRAISE

The conviction of sin is an evidence of genuine salvation. Praise God for the conviction of the Holy Spirit, the depth of His grace, and the joy of forgiveness.

PRAYER

Confession: Admit any sin that you have refused to acknowledge to the Lord. Remember that the blood of Christ will cover every sin that we are willing to uncover but that God will one day uncover every sin we insist on covering.

Supplication: Ask God to give you increasing sensitivity to the conviction of His Spirit, a heart that truly mourns over sin, and a desire to quickly confess and repent of all sin.

Intercession: Use this passage as a basis to pray for someone whom God places on your heart.

SING TO THE LORD

It Is Well With My Soul

When peace like a river attendeth my way,
When sorrows like sea billows roll;
Whatever my lot, Thou hast taught me to say,
"It is well, it is well with my soul."

My sin—O, the bliss of this glorious tho't—
My sin—not in part, but the whole,
Is nailed to the cross, and I bear it no more,
Praise the Lord, praise the Lord, O my soul!

And, Lord, haste the day when the faith shall be sight,
The clouds be rolled back as a scroll,
The trump shall resound and the Lord shall descend,
"Even so"—it is well with my soul.

It is well with my soul,
It is well, it is well with my soul.

HORATIO G. SPAFFORD

TAKE-AWAY THOUGHT

*What key thought, phrase, or verse from this psalm
will you take with you into your day?*

---

[1] Spurgeon, *Treasury of David*, 156.
[2] Ibid., 159.

Preparing Your Heart

Ask God to quiet your heart and to speak to you through His Word. Ask Him to shine the light of His truth into your life. In this quiet moment, surrender yourself to Him and commit to obey whatever He shows you. Begin your time of devotion with this prayer:

> *Open my eyes that I may see*
> *wonderful things in your law.*
> *Give me understanding, and I will keep your law*
> *and obey it with all my heart.*
> *Show me your ways, O Lord,*
> *teach me your paths;*
> *guide me in your truth and teach me,*
> *for you are God my Savior,*
> *and my hope is in you all day long.*
> *Teach me what I cannot see;*
> *if I have done wrong, I will not do so again.*

PSALM 119:18, 34; 25:4–5; JOB 34:32 NIV

$\mathscr{L}$istening to God

∞ Read Psalm 51 thoughtfully and prayerfully.

∞ What key words stand out to you in this passage?

∞ Write out a key verse from this passage.

∞ Summarize the entire passage in a sentence or two.

WHAT DOES THIS PASSAGE SAY?
(Observation)

1. What phrases in this psalm indicate that David didn't think he deserved God's forgiveness?

_____

_____

2. On what basis did David appeal to God for mercy and forgiveness (v. 1)?

_____

_____

3. What effect did guilt have on David (vv. 3, 8, 12, 13)?

_____

_____

4. What do we learn about the nature of sin from verses 4 and 5?

_____

_____

> "The essence of sin lies in its opposition to God. . . . David had wronged Bathsheba and Uriah, but his greatest misery was that he had offended his God. Graceless men care nothing about this."[1]
>
> CHARLES H. SPURGEON
>
> *Helpful Background*
>
> "When David spoke of God's cleansing him with hyssop, he was alluding to the use of hyssop at the religious ceremonies to sprinkle sacrificial blood on the altar. This represented the removal of sin through the shedding of blood (cf. Hebrews 9:22)."[2]

5. What evidences of genuine repentance do you see in this psalm (vv. 7–10, 12–15, 19)? What was David's attitude toward his sin, toward God, and toward himself as a sinner?

_____

_____

WHAT DOES THIS PASSAGE MEAN?
(Interpretation)

1. Why did David verbalize his sorrow and confession so specifically? Why is it important for us to confess our sins specifically?

_____

_____

2. Why is it vital that we see our sin as being committed "against God" (v. 4)?

_____

_____

3. What role does honesty play in our experiencing complete cleansing? What role does denial play in our remaining guilty (v. 6)?

_____

_____

4. How does repentance make us more useful to God (vv. 13, 15)?

_____

_____

HOW CAN I MAKE THIS PASSAGE A PART OF MY LIFE?
(Application)

1. When was the last time you confessed your sins to God with heartfelt sorrow? What unconfessed sin are you hiding in your heart now?

_____

_____

2. Have you allowed any sinful residue to linger in your mind from a past sin? Has your repentance been deep and thorough or surface-level and partial? What do you think God wants you to experience?

_____

_____

3. Do you ever tend to minimize your sin, rationalizing it as "not a big deal"? According to this passage, how should you view your sin?

_____

_____

4. Have you ever struggled with the sense that your sin is so great you could never be fully forgiven? What hope do you find in David's prayer?

_____

_____

5. On what basis can you plead for and claim God's mercy and forgiveness for your sin?

_____

_____

FOR FURTHER MEDITATION
Hebrews 10:19–23

$\mathscr{R}$esponding to God

PRAISE

Praise God for the blood of Christ shed on the cross to cover over your sin.

PRAYER

Confession: Spend some time with God, openly airing how you feel about your sin. Ask Him to give you deep, godly sorrow.

Supplication: Ask God to purify your heart, to wash you with the blood of Jesus, and to fill you with His Holy Spirit.

Intercession: Use one or more verses in this psalm as a basis to pray for someone you know who appears to be unrepentant over his or her sin.

SING TO THE LORD

Whiter Than Snow

Lord Jesus, I long to be perfectly whole;
I want You forever to live in my soul.
Break down every idol; cast out every foe—
Now wash me and I shall be whiter than snow.

Lord Jesus, look down from Your throne in the skies,
And help me to make a complete sacrifice.
I give up myself, and whatever I know—
Now wash me and I shall be whiter than snow.

Lord Jesus, for this I most humbly entreat;
I wait, blessed Lord, at Your crucified feet.
By faith, for my cleansing I see Your blood flow—
Now wash me and I shall be whiter than snow.

Lord Jesus, before You I patiently wait;
Come now, and within me a new heart create.
To those who have sought You, You never said "No"—
Now wash me and I shall be whiter than snow.

Whiter than snow, yes, whiter than snow;
Now wash me and I shall be whiter than snow.

JAMES NICHOLSON

TAKE-AWAY THOUGHT

*What key thought, phrase, or verse from this psalm
will you take with you into your day?*

1 *Spurgeon's Devotional Bible* (Grand Rapids: Baker Book House, 1976), 284.
2 John F. Walvoord and Roy B. Zuck, ed., *The Bible Knowledge Commentary* (USA: Victor Books, 1985), 832.

*P*salm 130

♡ *P*reparing Your Heart

Ask God to quiet your heart and to speak to you through His Word. Ask Him to shine the light of His truth into your life. In this quiet moment, surrender yourself to Him and commit to obey whatever He shows you. Begin your time of devotion with this prayer:

> *Open my eyes that I may see*
> *wonderful things in your law.*
> *Give me understanding, and I will keep your law*
> *and obey it with all my heart.*
> *Show me your ways, O Lord,*
> *teach me your paths;*
> *guide me in your truth and teach me,*
> *for you are God my Savior,*
> *and my hope is in you all day long.*
> *Teach me what I cannot see;*
> *if I have done wrong, I will not do so again.*
>
> PSALM 119:18, 34; 25:4–5; JOB 34:32 NIV

$\mathcal{L}$istening to God

∞ Read Psalm 130 thoughtfully and prayerfully.

∞ What key words stand out to you in this passage?

∞ Write out a key verse from this passage.

∞ Summarize the entire passage in a sentence or two.

WHAT DOES THIS PASSAGE SAY?
(Observation)

1. Where was the psalmist when he cried out to the Lord (v. 1)? How would you describe the tone of his prayer?

2. We don't know what specific circumstances ("depths") the psalmist was facing when he wrote this psalm. What is one possibility suggested by verse 3?

3. What does this passage suggest about the psalmist's heart attitude toward his sin?

4. What is the object of his hope (v. 5)?

_____

_____

WHAT DOES THIS PASSAGE MEAN?
(Interpretation)

1. Does verse 3 mean that God does not notice our sins?

_____

_____

2. Why is it impossible for sinners to stand before God (v. 3)? What is the only way that sinners can stand before God (v. 4)?

_____

_____

> "The psalmist recognized that no one could stand if God dealt with sinners according to what they deserved. To 'mark' (keep a record of) sins means to hold one accountable for his sins. The comfort is that with God there is forgiveness (. . . 'pardon' . . .). This is the reason for the Lord's not keeping records of sins; He forgives. Believers throughout all ages have rejoiced over this fact, for apart from this, none could endure His judgment!"[1]

3. How does God's forgiveness lead to greater fear of the Lord (v. 4)?

_____

_____

> "God forgives so that the forgiven will fear Him. This general word for fear often includes the ideas of worship and obedience. . . . The forgiveness of God cannot be treated lightly. It turns sinners into saints, people who follow Him in obedience."[2]

4. Why is God's Word a basis for confidence and hope?

5. What image does the psalmist use to describe the way he waits for the Lord? What does that analogy suggest about what it means to wait on the Lord?

6. What does this passage teach about God's supply of mercy (vv. 7–8)?

HOW CAN I MAKE THIS PASSAGE A PART OF MY LIFE?
(Application)

1. When the psalmist experienced the weight and guilt of his sin, he cried out to the Lord, who was his only hope. Where else do some people look for relief from guilt and condemnation?

2. Are you placing your hope completely in the Lord and in His Word? Do you tend to trust something or someone else to meet your earthly and eternal needs?

.On what basis alone can you be assured of God's forgiveness for your sins?

_____

_____

.How could this psalm be used to explain the gospel to an unbeliever? What key words in this passage could be used as an outline for the gospel?

_____

_____

FOR FURTHER MEDITATION

Romans 8:1; 1 Peter 1:17–19; Romans 8:23

*R*esponding to God

PRAISE

Praise God for the fullness of His mercy, His forgiveness, and His redemption.

PRAYER

Confession: Meditate on verse 3. Humbly acknowledge your need for God's mercy.

Supplication: Express your desire to walk in the fear of the Lord, trusting and hoping in Him alone.

Intercession: Use this passage as a basis to pray for someone whom God places on your heart.

SING TO THE LORD

Grace Greater Than Our Sin

Marvelous grace of our loving Lord,
    grace that exceeds our sin and our guilt,
Yonder on Calvary's mount outpoured,
    there where the blood of the Lamb was spilt.

Sin and despair, like the sea waves cold,
    threaten the soul with infinite loss;
Grace that is greater, yes, grace untold,
    points to the refuge, the mighty cross.

Dark is the stain that we cannot hide—
    what can avail to wash it away?
Look! There is flowing a crimson tide;
    whiter than snow you may be today.

Marvelous, infinite, matchless grace,
    freely bestowed on all who believe!
You who are longing to see His face,
    will you this moment His grace receive?

    Grace, grace, God's grace,
        grace that will pardon and cleanse within!
    Grace, grace, God's grace,
        grace that is greater than all our sin!

JULIA H. JOHNSON

TAKE-AWAY THOUGHT

*What key thought, phrase, or verse from this psalm
will you take with you into your day?*

---

[1] Walvoord and Zuck, 886.

[2] Ibid.

Psalm 143

Preparing Your Heart

Ask God to quiet your heart and to speak to you through His Word. Ask Him to shine the light of His truth into your life. In this quiet moment, surrender yourself to Him and commit to obey whatever He shows you. Begin your time of devotion with this prayer:

> *Open my eyes that I may see*
> *wonderful things in your law.*
> *Give me understanding, and I will keep your law*
> *and obey it with all my heart.*
> *Show me your ways, O Lord,*
> *teach me your paths;*
> *guide me in your truth and teach me,*
> *for you are God my Savior,*
> *and my hope is in you all day long.*
> *Teach me what I cannot see;*
> *if I have done wrong, I will not do so again.*
>
> PSALM 119:18, 34; 25:4–5; JOB 34:32 NIV

Listening to God

- Read Psalm 143 thoughtfully and prayerfully.
- What key words stand out to you in this passage?

- Write out a key verse from this passage.

- Summarize the entire passage in a sentence or two.

WHAT DOES THIS PASSAGE SAY?
(Observation)

1. On what basis does David plead with God to hear his prayer (vv. 1, 11–12)?

2. What verse indicates that David is approaching God as a repentant sinner?

> *"We have no righteousness of our own to plead, and therefore must plead God's righteousness. . . . David, before he prays for the removal of his trouble, prays for the pardon of his sin, and depends upon mere mercy for it."*[1]
> MATTHEW HENRY

3. How does David describe his desperate condition (vv. 3–4, 6, 7)? What is he facing?

_____

_____

4. What petition in David's prayer expresses his desire to *know* the will of God? What request expresses his desire to *obey* the will of God?

_____

_____

5. David's great need prompts fervent prayer. In verses 7–12, he makes eleven petitions, one right after the next. What are those petitions? (Each verse contains two, except for verse 9, which has only one.)

_____

_____

6. What makes David so confident that God can be trusted in the midst of his distress?

_____

_____

WHAT DOES THIS PASSAGE MEAN?
(Interpretation)

1. How can meditating on what God has done in the past encourage us in times of distress (v. 5)?

_____

_____

"To recall our past is to promote sadness, very often, or self-pity; to recall the Lord's past prompts confident prayer." [2]

2.Why is it important to "hear" God's voice in the morning (v. 8)?

_____

_____

3.How can pressures and distressing circumstances actually be a blessing?

_____

_____

HOW CAN I MAKE THIS PASSAGE A PART OF MY LIFE?
(Application)

1.The "enemies" that overwhelm us and persecute our souls can be physical, emotional, mental, or spiritual; external or internal; seen or unseen. What are some of the enemies in your life? Circle the enemies on your list that you are currently struggling against.

_____

_____

2.Do you ever experience feelings of condemnation over your sin? If you are a child of God, where do those thoughts come from? How can you escape them?

_____

_____

3. Twice in this psalm, David refers to himself as "Your servant" (vv. 2, 12). Would you readily call yourself God's servant? How should that recognition affect the way you think, live, and pray?

_____

_____

4. Where do you tend to take shelter when you are under pressure? How can you cultivate the habit of taking refuge in God?

_____

_____

FOR FURTHER MEDITATION

Romans 3:20–24

$\mathcal{R}$esponding to God

PRAISE

Praise God for His righteousness that has been credited to your account through faith in Christ.

PRAYER

Confession: Admit your inability to please God and your total unrighteousness apart from Christ.

Supplication: Pray through David's petitions in verses 7–12, personalizing them for your own life.

Intercession: Use this passage as a basis to pray for someone whom God places on your heart.

SING TO THE LORD

Have Thine Own Way, Lord!

Have Thine own way, Lord! Have Thine own way!
Thou art the Potter; I am the clay.
Mold me and make me after Thy will,
While I am waiting, yielded and still.

Have Thine own way, Lord! Have Thine own way!
Search me and try me, Master, today.
Whiter than snow, Lord, wash me just now,
As in Thy presence humbly I bow.

Have Thine own way, Lord! Have Thine own way!
Hold o'er my being absolute sway!
Fill with Thy Spirit till all shall see
Christ only, always living in me!

ADELAIDE A. POLLARD

TAKE-AWAY THOUGHT

*What key thought, phrase, or verse from this psalm
will you take with you into your day?*

[1] Henry, 726–7.

[2] D. A. Carson, et al., ed., *New Bible Commentary*, 21st Century Edition (Downers Grove, IL: Intervarsity Press, 1994), 580.

Psalm 34

Preparing Your Heart

Ask God to quiet your heart and to speak to you through His Word. Ask Him to shine the light of His truth into your life. In this quiet moment, surrender yourself to Him and commit to obey whatever He shows you. Begin your time of devotion with this prayer:

Open my eyes that I may see
wonderful things in your law.
Give me understanding, and I will keep your law
and obey it with all my heart.
Show me your ways, O Lord,
teach me your paths;
guide me in your truth and teach me,
for you are God my Savior,
and my hope is in you all day long.
Teach me what I cannot see;
if I have done wrong, I will not do so again.

PSALM 119:18, 34; 25:4–5; JOB 34:32 NIV

$\mathscr{L}$istening to God

- Read Psalm 34 thoughtfully and prayerfully.

- What key words stand out to you in this passage?

- Write out a key verse from this passage.

- Summarize the entire passage in a sentence or two.

WHAT DOES THIS PASSAGE SAY?
(Observation)

1. Read the title of the psalm and 1 Samuel 21:10–15 to understand the context of this psalm. Briefly describe David's situation. How did he choose to respond?

2. List all the words or phrases that you can find in this psalm that tell us what our attitude and actions should be toward the Lord (e.g., bless Him, praise Him).

3. List three or four blessings that are given to the righteous (meaning those who have a right relationship with God and are committed to righteous living).

_____

_____

4. What are the characteristics of a person who fears the Lord (vv. 9–14)?

_____

_____

5. What are the qualifications or conditions that must be met in order for Him to hear our cries and deliver us (vv. 15–18)?

_____

_____

6. How are the righteous and the wicked contrasted (vv. 15–22)?

_____

_____

WHAT DOES THIS PASSAGE MEAN?
(Interpretation)

1. When we "magnify the Lord," how do our pressures and problems appear different?

_____

_____

2. How does David use his personal testimony to touch the lives of others in need (vv. 1–11)?

_____

_____

3. How is immediate, temporal relief different from ultimate, eternal deliverance? Which is more important? Why might God sometimes choose to *not* deliver us from our immediate problems?

_____

_____

4. Verses 6, 15, and 17 speak of "crying out" to the Lord. Why do you think it is important to cry out to God when we are in trouble?

_____

_____

"I sought the Lord, and He heard me. God expects to hear from you before you can expect to hear from Him. If you restrain prayer, it is no wonder the mercy promised is retained."[1]

WILLIAM GURNALL

HOW CAN I MAKE THIS PASSAGE A PART OF MY LIFE?
(Application)

1. Which promises in this psalm are particularly encouraging to you?

_____

_____

2. What are some of the troubles God has delivered you out of?

_____

_____

3. David made a determined choice to praise the Lord in every circumstance, as an act of his will: "I will bless the Lord at all times" (v. 1). Write a short statement of commitment to God, choosing to bless Him at all times.

_____

_____

4. Do you know anyone who is going through a difficult time? How can you encourage your friend? What can you share from your own experience about how God has met your needs in the past?

_____

_____

FOR FURTHER MEDITATION

Philippians 4:4–7; 2 Corinthians 1:8–11

$\mathscr{R}$esponding to God

PRAISE

Personalize the phrases of protection and blessing that you found in this psalm, and thank Him for how He cares for you.

PRAYER

Confession: Acknowledge the times when you have failed to bless and trust the Lord in the midst of your problems.

Supplication: Cry out to the Lord about whatever difficult circumstances you are facing in your life at this time. Ask Him to help you praise His name in the midst of your circumstances.

Intercession: Use this passage as a basis to pray for someone whom God places on your heart.

SING TO THE LORD

O For a Thousand Tongues To Sing

O for a thousand tongues to sing my great Redeemer's praise,
The glories of my God and King, the triumphs of His grace.

Jesus! The name that charms our fears, that bids our sorrows cease,
'Tis music in the sinner's ears, 'tis life and health and peace.

He breaks the pow'r of cancelled sin, he sets the prisoner free;
His blood can make the foulest clean; His blood availed for me.

Hear Him, ye deaf; His praise, ye dumb, your loosened tongues employ;
Ye blind, behold your Savior come; and leap, ye lame, for joy.

My gracious Master and my God, assist me to proclaim,
To spread thro' all the earth abroad, the honors of Thy name.

CHARLES WESLEY

TAKE-AWAY THOUGHT

*What key thought, phrase, or verse from this psalm
will you take with you into your day?*

---

[1] Spurgeon, *Treasury of David*, 165.

Psalm 36

*P*reparing Your Heart

Ask God to quiet your heart and to speak to you through His Word. Ask Him to shine the light of His truth into your life. In this quiet moment, surrender yourself to Him and commit to obey whatever He shows you. Begin your time of devotion with this prayer:

> *Open my eyes that I may see*
> *wonderful things in your law.*
> *Give me understanding, and I will keep your law*
> *and obey it with all my heart.*
> *Show me your ways, O Lord,*
> *teach me your paths;*
> *guide me in your truth and teach me,*
> *for you are God my Savior,*
> *and my hope is in you all day long.*
> *Teach me what I cannot see;*
> *if I have done wrong, I will not do so again.*
>
> PSALM 119:18, 34; 25:4–5; JOB 34:32 NIV

ℒistening to God

- Read Psalm 36 thoughtfully and prayerfully.
- What key words stand out to you in this passage?

- Write out a key verse from this passage.

- Summarize the entire passage in a sentence or two.

WHAT DOES THIS PASSAGE SAY?
(Observation)

1. How do verses 1–4 describe the character, the communication, and the conduct of the wicked?

2. In one phrase, what is the fundamental problem of the wicked?

> "Wickedness is the fruit of an atheistic root. If God be everywhere, and I fear Him, how can I dare to break His laws in His very presence? . . . God-fearing men see their sins and bewail them. Where the reverse is the case, we may be sure there is no fear of God."[1]
>
> CHARLES H. SPURGEON

3. What images does the psalmist use to communicate that God is immense and immeasurable, unmovable and unfathomable?

_____

_____

4. What do verses 6–8 reveal about God's relationship and dealings with His people?

_____

_____

5. What is the appropriate response to this kind of God (vv. 7–9)?

_____

_____

WHAT DOES THIS PASSAGE MEAN?
(Interpretation)

1. How does a lack of the fear of the Lord result in other sins?

_____

_____

"He who makes little of God makes much of himself. They who forget adoration fall into adulation. The eyes must see something, and if they admire not God, they will flatter self."[2]

CHARLES H. SPURGEON

2. The word translated *fear* in verse 1 suggests "dread" or "terror." Why is it important to have a healthy dread or terror of the Lord? How can the fear of the Lord protect us and motivate us?

_____

_____

3. What is the only true source of abundance and fullness, of life and light (vv. 8–9)?

_____

_____

4. What does it mean to "see light" in "Your light" (v. 9)?

_____

_____

Spotlight on a Word

The Hebrew word *hesed* is used three times in this psalm (vv. 5, 7, 10). Depending on the translation you are using, this word may be rendered "mercy," "lovingkindness," "kindness," or "love." It is one of the most important words in the Old Testament. It is a difficult word to translate because there is not a single English word that adequately communicates its full meaning. When used of God, *hesed* speaks of His loyal, unfailing love for His people—a love that flows out of a covenant relationship. Even though we may prove unfaithful to this covenant, His covenant love never ends; His *hesed* is everlasting.

5. Why do you think the psalmist considers God's *hesed* so precious?

_____

_____

HOW CAN I MAKE THIS PASSAGE A PART OF MY LIFE?
(Application)

6. Read carefully through each of the phrases that describe a wicked man in verses 1–4. Do any of these phrases describe you?

_____

_____

7. Can you detect a true sense of the fear of the Lord in your life? How does it change the way you think and act? How can you cultivate the fear of the Lord?

8. What does God's *hesed* mean to you? Why is it such a great gift?

FOR FURTHER MEDITATION
1 John 1:5b–7; 4:7–8; 5:11b–12

$\mathcal{R}$esponding to God

PRAISE

What does this passage teach you about God? Personalize the psalmist's words in verses 5–9, making this your own prayer of praise.

PRAYER

Confession: Repent of any ways that you have "flattered yourself in your own eyes."

Supplication: Ask God to make your life a reflection of His character as it is revealed in this psalm. Pray for protection against any pride or unrighteousness in your heart (v. 11).

Intercession: Use this passage as a basis to pray for someone whom God places on your heart.

SING TO THE LORD

Immortal, Invisible, God Only Wise

Immortal, invisible, God only wise,
In light inaccessible hid from our eyes.
Most blessed, most glorious, the Ancient of Days,
Almighty, victorious—Thy great name we praise.

Unresting, unhasting, and silent as light,
Nor wanting, nor wasting, Thou rulest in might;
Thy justice, like mountains, high soaring above
Thy clouds, which are fountains of goodness and love.

To all, life Thou givest—to both great and small;
In all life Thou livest—the true life of all.
Thy wisdom so boundless, Thy mercy so free,
Eternal Thy goodness for naught changeth Thee.

Great Father of glory, pure Father of light,
Thine angels adore Thee, all veiling their sight;
All praise we would render—O help us to see
'Tis only the splendor of light hideth Thee!

WALTER CHALMERS SMITH

TAKE-AWAY THOUGHT

*What key thought, phrase, or verse from this psalm
will you take with you into your day?*

---

1 Spurgeon, *Treasury of David*, 174.
2 Ibid.

Psalm 66

❤ *P*reparing Your Heart

Ask God to quiet your heart and to speak to you through His Word. Ask Him to shine the light of His truth into your life. In this quiet moment, surrender yourself to Him and commit to obey whatever He shows you. Begin your time of devotion with this prayer:

> *Open my eyes that I may see*
> *wonderful things in your law.*
> *Give me understanding, and I will keep your law*
> *and obey it with all my heart.*
> *Show me your ways, O Lord,*
> *teach me your paths;*
> *guide me in your truth and teach me,*
> *for you are God my Savior,*
> *and my hope is in you all day long.*
> *Teach me what I cannot see;*
> *if I have done wrong, I will not do so again.*
>
> PSALM 119:18, 34; 25:4–5; JOB 34:32 NIV

ℒistening to God

- Read Psalm 66 thoughtfully and prayerfully.

- What key words stand out to you in this passage?

- Write out a key verse from this passage.

- Summarize the entire passage in a sentence or two.

WHAT DOES THIS PASSAGE SAY?
(Observation)

1. In verses 1–5, the psalmist focuses on "all the earth." How has God shown Himself to all humanity?

_____

_____

2. How should the whole earth respond to God?

_____

_____

3. In verses 6–12, the focus shifts to the redeemed people of God. (Note the pronouns "we," "our," and "us.") The psalmist reminds the redeemed of the crossing of the Red Sea (out of Egypt) and the Jordan River (into the Promised Land). What is the appropriate response to such memories (vv. 6–7)?

4. He then reminds them of God's other actions on their behalf (vv. 9–12). How would you describe those actions?

> *"We, too, often forget that God lays our afflictions upon us; if we remembered this fact, we should more patiently submit to the pressure which now pains us. The time will come when, for every ounce of present burden, we shall receive a far more exceeding and eternal weight of glory."* [1]
>
> CHARLES H. SPURGEON

5. In verses 13–20, the focus becomes personal. (Note the pronouns "I" and "my.") How does the psalmist express gratitude to God for answered prayer (vv. 13–15)? How does he express that gratitude to others (vv. 16–20)?

6. What role does a pure heart play in prayer?

WHAT DOES THIS PASSAGE MEAN?
(Interpretation)

7. Why is it important to remember our "redemptive past" and to recall God's saving work on our behalf?

8. According to verses 8–12, what is God's purpose in taking us through difficult circumstances? What will be the ultimate outcome of such trials?

"He imposes purposeful sufferings in which [his people] are tested for quality and refined for purity; he appoints all our experiences, however dreadful. When life hems us in (prison), when pressures mount (burdens), when people are atrociously cruel (ride roughshod), when one threatening circumstance follows hard on another (fire . . . water)—it is all his personal act: we are never elsewhere than in our Father's hand (Jn 10:29; 1 Cor 10:13)."[2]

HOW CAN I MAKE THIS PASSAGE A PART OF MY LIFE?
(Application)

1. How has God used affliction in your life to test and refine you? What fruit has it brought, or will it bring, in your life?

---

2. After experiencing God's deliverance, the psalmist offers sacrifices to express his gratitude and devotion to God. What are some ways you can express your gratitude for what God has done for you?

---

3. The psalmist is eager to share with others what God has done for him (v. 16). What has God done in your life lately? With whom can you share that testimony?

"We should take all occasions to tell one another of the great things which God has done for our souls, the spiritual blessings with which he has blessed us."[3]

MATTHEW HENRY

FOR FURTHER MEDITATION

James 1:2–4; 1 Peter 4:12–13; Romans 8:18

*R*esponding to God

PRAISE

Thank the Lord for the way He has used trials to test and refine you. Praise Him for His promise to bring you through those trials into a place of fulfillment.

PRAYER

Confession: Admit any sin that you have been holding on to in your heart.

Supplication: Ask God to give you a submissive heart toward Him—a heart that openly receives whatever He brings into your life.

Intercession: Pray for another believer you know who is going through a time of testing. Pray that God will use this time to strengthen him or her.

SING TO THE LORD

Come, Thou Fount of Every Blessing

Come, Thou Fount of every blessing, tune my heart to sing Thy grace;
Streams of mercy, never ceasing, call for songs of loudest praise.
Teach me some melodious sonnet, sung by flaming tongues above;
Praise His name—I'm fixed upon it—name of God's redeeming love.

Hitherto Thy love has blest me; Thou hast bro't me to this place;
And I know Thy hand will bring me safely home by Thy good grace.
Jesus sought me when a stranger, wand'ring from the fold of God;
He, to rescue me from danger, bo't me with His precious blood.

O to grace how great a debtor daily I'm constrained to be!
Let Thy goodness, like a fetter, bind my wand'ring heart to Thee:
Prone to wander, Lord, I feel it, prone to leave the God I love;
Here's my heart, O take and seal it; seal it for Thy courts above.

ROBERT ROBINSON

ADAPTED BY MARGARET CLARKSON

TAKE-AWAY THOUGHT

*What key thought, phrase, or verse from this psalm
will you take with you into your day?*

[1] Spurgeon, *Treasury of David*, 284.
[2] *New Bible Commentary*, 526.
[3] Henry, 645.

$\mathscr{P}$salm 92

$\mathscr{P}$reparing Your Heart

Ask God to quiet your heart and to speak to you through His Word. Ask Him to shine the light of His truth into your life. In this quiet moment, surrender yourself to Him and commit to obey whatever He shows you. Begin your time of devotion with this prayer:

> Open my eyes that I may see
> wonderful things in your law.
> Give me understanding, and I will keep your law
> and obey it with all my heart.
> Show me your ways, O Lord,
> teach me your paths;
> guide me in your truth and teach me,
> for you are God my Savior,
> and my hope is in you all day long.
> Teach me what I cannot see;
> if I have done wrong, I will not do so again.
>
> PSALM 119:18, 34; 25:4–5; JOB 34:32 NIV

159

$\mathscr{L}$istening to God

- Read Psalm 92 thoughtfully and prayerfully.
- What key words stand out to you in this passage?

- Write out a key verse from this passage.

- Summarize the entire passage in a sentence or two.

WHAT DOES THIS PASSAGE SAY?
(Observation)

1. Based on the title and verse 1, what should be the "work" of the Lord's Day?

2. What does this psalm reveal about God (vv. 1, 5, 8, 15)?

3. What image does the psalmist use to describe the wicked (v. 7)? What images does he use to describe the righteous (v. 12)? How do those images compare?

.What is the destiny of God's enemies (vv. 6, 7, 9)? What is the destiny of the righteous (vv. 4, 10–15)?

_____

_____

.What two particular attributes of God should we praise every day (v. 2)?

_____

_____

Spotlight on a Word

Faithfulness translates a Hebrew word that speaks of firmness, steadiness, steadfastness, trust, honesty, and certainty. It is closely related to the word Amen, meaning sure, truly.[1]

"Every night, clouded or clear, moonlit or dark, calm or tempestuous, is alike suitable for a song upon the faithfulness of God, since in all seasons, and under all circumstances, it abides the same."[2]

CHARLES H. SPURGEON

WHAT DOES THIS PASSAGE MEAN?
(Interpretation)

.How can God's works be a source of gladness for His people (v. 4)?

_____

_____

.In what ways are the righteous like a tree?

_____

_____

"The trees of righteousness do not grow of themselves; they are planted, not in common soil, but in the house of the Lord. Trees are not usually planted in a house; but God's trees are said to be planted in his house because it is from his grace, by his word and Spirit, that they receive all the sap and virtue that keep them alive and make them fruitful. . . . The wicked flourish as the grass (v. 7), which is soon withered, but the righteous as the palm-tree, which is long-lived and which the winter does not change."[3]

MATTHEW HENRY

3. According to verse 13, what is the best environment for spiritual growth and fruitfulness? Practically, how can believers live in that environment?

HOW CAN I MAKE THIS PASSAGE A PART OF MY LIFE?
(Application)

1. How do you honor the Lord's Day as a special day? What can you do to set apart that day to the Lord?

2. Have you made praise a part of your lifestyle? Before you go to sleep tonight, praise God for His faithfulness through the day. When you awake in the morning, thank Him for His lovingkindness (His unfailing, covenant love).

3. The psalmist tells us that it is good to sing praises to God's name. Choose a song to sing aloud to God now.

FOR FURTHER MEDITATION
Revelation 15:3–4

*R*esponding to God

PRAISE

Thank the Lord for His lovingkindness and His faithfulness.

PRAYER

Confession: Acknowledge any sin that God brings to mind as you allow Him to search your heart.

Supplication: Express to God your desire to live in His presence, to flourish spiritually, and to be fruitful all your life.

Intercession: Pray for some of "God's enemies." Pray that they will be brought to repentance before it is too late.

SING TO THE LORD

Praise to the Lord, the Almighty

Praise to the Lord, the Almighty, the King of creation!
O my soul, praise Him, for He is thy health and salvation!
All ye who hear, now to His temple draw near;
Join me in glad adoration!

Praise to the Lord, who o'er all things so wondrously reigneth,
Shelters thee under His wings, yea, so gently sustaineth!
Hast thou not seen how thy desires all have been
Granted in what He ordaineth?

Praise to the Lord! O let all that is in me adore Him!
All that hath life and breath, come now with praises before Him!
Let the "amen" sound from His people again;
Gladly forever adore Him!

JOACHIM NEANDER

TRANSLATED BY CATHERINE WINKWORTH

TAKE-AWAY THOUGHT

*What key thought, phrase, or verse from this psalm
will you take with you into your day?*

---

[1] *Word Study Old Testament,* 2301.

[2] Spurgeon, *Treasury of David,* 388.

[3] Henry, *Commentary,* 679.

Psalm 103

Preparing Your Heart

Ask God to quiet your heart and to speak to you through His Word. Ask Him to shine the light of His truth into your life. In this quiet moment, surrender yourself to Him and commit to obey whatever He shows you. Begin your time of devotion with this prayer:

> *Open my eyes that I may see*
> *wonderful things in your law.*
> *Give me understanding, and I will keep your law*
> *and obey it with all my heart.*
> *Show me your ways, O Lord,*
> *teach me your paths;*
> *guide me in your truth and teach me,*
> *for you are God my Savior,*
> *and my hope is in you all day long.*
> *Teach me what I cannot see;*
> *if I have done wrong, I will not do so again.*
>
> PSALM 119:18, 34; 25:4–5; JOB 34:32 NIV

ℒistening to God

- Read Psalm 103 thoughtfully and prayerfully.
- What key words stand out to you in this passage?

- Write out a key verse from this passage.

- Summarize the entire passage in a sentence or two.

WHAT DOES THIS PASSAGE SAY?
(Observation)

Bless the Lord, O my soul;

And all that is within me, bless His holy name!

PSALM 103:1

FOR FURTHER INSIGHT

"When the Lord 'blesses' us, he reviews our needs and responds to them; when we 'bless' the Lord, we review his excellencies and respond to them. . . . We 'bless' the Lord himself before we recount his blessings. All he does stems from who he is (name) and what he is (holy)."[1]

1. In verses 3–5, David blesses the Lord for His many benefits. List the benefits for which he expresses gratitude.

_____

_____

2. What do verses 6–19 reveal about God?

_____

_____

3. How should we respond to a God like this (vv. 1–2, 13, 17, 18, 20–21)?

_____

_____

4. In verses 20–22, all creation is exhorted to join together in a great chorus of praise. Who are the participants in this universal choir?

_____

_____

WHAT DOES THIS PASSAGE MEAN?
(Interpretation)

1. What does it mean to bless the Lord?

_____

_____

2. How can we bless the Lord with all that is within us?

_____

_____

3. Why is it important to know the history of God's dealings with His people (v. 7)?

_____

_____

4. In this psalm, David keeps coming back to God's redemptive work of mercy, forgiveness, and grace toward sinners. What does this passage teach us about how God deals with our sin? Why is this cause for such exuberant praise?

"'Who forgiveth all thine iniquities.' It is not some or 'many of thine iniquities.' This would never do. If so much as the very smallest iniquity in thought, word, or act, were left unforgiven, we should be just as badly off, just as far from God, just as unfit for heaven, just as exposed to hell, as though the whole weight of our sins were yet upon us. . . . When God cancels a man's sins, He does so according to the measure in which Christ bore those sins. Now, Christ not only bore some or many of the believer's sins, He bore them all, and, therefore, God forgives all."[2]

CHARLES H. SPURGEON

5. How should the way God deals with us affect the way we treat others (vv. 8–14)?

HOW CAN I MAKE THIS PASSAGE A PART OF MY LIFE?
(Application)

1. David highlights the mercies he has received from the Lord. What are some material blessings He has given you? What are some spiritual, eternal blessings?

2. What kind of attitudes, words, or actions might result from failing to bless the Lord?

_____

_____

3. David talks with his own heart about the mercies of God. Try writing your own psalm of praise, beginning the same way David does. *Bless the Lord, O my soul; and all that is within me, bless His holy name! Bless the Lord, O my soul, and forget not all His benefits . . .*

_____

_____

FOR FURTHER MEDITATION

Ephesians 1:3, 7

*R*esponding to God

PRAISE

Bless the Lord for His incredible mercy, grace, and forgiveness.

PRAYER

Confession: Agree with God that you deserve eternal punishment for your sins.

Supplication: Ask God to give you a heart that is always conscious of His blessings and quick to express gratitude.

Intercession: Use this passage as a basis to pray for someone whom God places on your heart.

SING TO THE LORD

Praise My Soul, the King of Heaven

Praise my soul, the King of heaven; to His feet your tribute bring.
Ransomed, healed, restored, forgiven, evermore His praises sing.
Alleluia! Alleluia! Praise the everlasting King!

Praise Him for His grace and favor to our fathers in distress;
Praise Him, still the same as ever, slow to chide and swift to bless.
Alleluia! Alleluia! Glorious in His faithfulness!

Father-like, He tends and spares us; well our feeble frame He knows.
In His hands He gently bears us, rescues us from all our foes.
Alleluia! Alleluia! Widely yet His mercy flows.

Angels in the height, adore Him; you behold Him face to face.
Saints triumphant, bow before Him; gathered in from every race.
Alleluia! Alleluia! Praise with us the God of grace!

HENRY F. LYTE

TAKE-AWAY THOUGHT

*What key thought, phrase, or verse from this psalm
will you take with you into your day?*

[1] *New Bible Commentary*, 552.
[2] Spurgeon, *Treasury of David*, 425.

Psalm 116

♡ *P*reparing Your Heart

Ask God to quiet your heart and to speak to you through His Word. Ask Him to shine the light of His truth into your life. In this quiet moment, surrender yourself to Him and commit to obey whatever He shows you. Begin your time of devotion with this prayer:

Open my eyes that I may see
  wonderful things in your law.
Give me understanding, and I will keep your law
  and obey it with all my heart.
Show me your ways, O Lord,
  teach me your paths;
guide me in your truth and teach me,
  for you are God my Savior,
  and my hope is in you all day long.
Teach me what I cannot see;
  if I have done wrong, I will not do so again.

PSALM 119:18, 34; 25:4–5; JOB 34:32 NIV

171

Listening to God

∞   Read Psalm 116 thoughtfully and prayerfully.

∞   What key words stand out to you in this passage?

∞   Write out a key verse from this passage.

∞   Summarize the entire passage in a sentence or two.

WHAT DOES THIS PASSAGE SAY?
(Observation)

In a Nutshell

"Personal love fostered by a personal experience of redemption is the theme of this Psalm, and in it we see the redeemed answered when they pray, preserved in time of trouble, resting in their God, walking at large, sensible of their obligations, conscious that they are not their own but bought with a price, and joining with all the ransomed company to sing hallelujahs unto God."[1]

CHARLES H. SPURGEON

1. What did the psalmist do when he was in peril of death (v. 4)?

_____

_____

Spotlight on a Word

Call: "to cry out, call aloud, roar; summon; implore. . . . It is usually addressed to a specific recipient and intended to elicit a specific response. Rarely does it refer to a random outcry. . . . [To call] upon the name of God, i.e., to summon His aid. Usually the context has to do with a critical . . . or chronic need."[2]

2. What did the psalmist learn about the nature and ways of God from his personal experience (vv. 1, 5–7, 16)?

_____

_____

3. What kind of person does God save (v. 6)?

_____

_____

4. What did the psalmist purpose to do as an expression of gratitude for God's intervention?

(v. 1) _____

(vv. 2, 13, 17) _____

(v. 7) _____

(v. 9) _____

(vv. 13–15, 17–19) _____

(v. 16) _____

WHAT DOES THIS PASSAGE MEAN?
(Interpretation)

1. What are the similarities between the psalmist's deliverance from physical death and the believer's salvation from spiritual death (vv. 3–8)?

_____

_____

173

2. The psalmist pledges to pay his vows to the Lord "in the presence of all His people" (vv. 14, 18). Why is it important to offer public praise and testimony of God's deliverance?

___

"God's praise is not to be confined to a closet, nor His Name to be whispered in holes and corners, as if we were afraid that men should hear us; but in the thick of the throng, and in the very center of assemblies, we should lift up heart and voice unto the Lord and invite others to join with us in adoring Him."[3]

CHARLES H. SPURGEON

3. In what sense is every believer both free and a slave? (See v. 16; Romans 6:16–18, 22.)

___

"Thou hast made me free, and I am impatient to be bound again. Thou hast broken the bonds of sin; now, Lord, bind me with the cords of love. Thou hast delivered me from the tyranny of Satan; make me as one of Thy hired servants. I owe my liberty, my life, and all that I have, or hope, to Thy generous rescue: and now, O my gracious, my divine Friend and Redeemer, I lay myself and my all at Thy feet."[4]

SAMUEL LAVINGTON

HOW CAN I MAKE THIS PASSAGE A PART OF MY LIFE?
(Application)

1. How would you finish the following sentence (based on verse 1)? "I love the Lord, because . . . "

___

..Both the Old and New Testaments contain the wonderful promise, "Whoever calls on the name of the Lord shall be saved" (Joel 2:32; Acts 2:21; Romans 10:13). Have you ever called on the name of the Lord to save you from your sin? What do you remember about that time in your life?

_____

_____

3. What did He save you from? According to Psalm 116, what is an appropriate response to Him for hearing your call and delivering you from eternal death?

_____

_____

4. "You have loosed my bonds" (v. 16). What bonds has the Lord loosed in your life? In what areas of your life has He set you free? (See Romans 6:7–14, if you need some help.)

_____

_____

5. How can you publicly declare what God has done in your life?

_____

_____

FOR FURTHER MEDITATION

John 5:24; Hebrews 13:15

$\mathscr{R}$esponding to God

PRAISE

Express your love to the Lord. Thank Him for saving you from sin and spiritual death. Thank Him for hearing and answering when you call on His name.

PRAYER

Confession: Admit to God any ways that you have taken His goodness for granted.

Supplication: Ask the Lord to help you call upon Him, walk in humility and obedience before Him, rest in Him, serve Him, and praise Him publicly.

Intercession: Use this passage as a basis to pray for someone whom God places on your heart.

SING TO THE LORD

Love Lifted Me

I was sinking deep in sin, far from the peaceful shore,
Very deeply stained within, sinking to rise no more;
But the Master of the sea heard my despairing cry,
From the waters lifted me—now safe am I.

> *Love lifted me! Love lifted me!*
> *When nothing else could help, love lifted me!*

All my heart to Him I give; ever to Him I'll cling,
In His blessed presence live, ever His praises sing.
Love so mighty and so true merits my soul's best songs;
Faithful, loving service, too, to Him belongs.

Souls in danger, look above; Jesus completely saves;
He will lift you by His love out of the angry waves.
He's the Master of the sea, billows His will obey;
He your Savior wants to be—be saved today.

JAMES ROWE

[1] Spurgeon, *Treasury of David*, 496.
[2] *Word Study Old Testament*, 2362.
[3] Spurgeon, *Treasury of David*, 501.
[4] Ibid.

Psalm 138

Preparing Your Heart

Ask God to quiet your heart and to speak to you through His Word. Ask Him to shine the light of His truth into your life. In this quiet moment, surrender yourself to Him and commit to obey whatever He shows you. Begin your time of devotion with this prayer:

> *Open my eyes that I may see*
> *wonderful things in your law.*
> *Give me understanding, and I will keep your law*
> *and obey it with all my heart.*
> *Show me your ways, O Lord,*
> *teach me your paths;*
> *guide me in your truth and teach me,*
> *for you are God my Savior,*
> *and my hope is in you all day long.*
> *Teach me what I cannot see;*
> *if I have done wrong, I will not do so again.*
>
> PSALM 119:18, 34; 25:4–5; JOB 34:32 NIV

$\mathscr{L}$istening to God

- Read Psalm 138 thoughtfully and prayerfully.
- What key words stand out to you in this passage?

- Write out a key verse from this passage.

- Summarize the entire passage in a sentence or two.

WHAT DOES THIS PASSAGE SAY?
(Observation)

1. For what does David praise God in each of the following verses?

   v. 2?

   v. 3?

   v. 6?

   v. 7?

   v. 8?

2. Even though David is in the midst of trouble (v. 7), he begins his prayer with praise and worship. How does each of the following help him to praise God when he is in troubled circumstances?

   Past experiences (v. 3)?

   Assurance of God's ultimate worldwide triumph (vv. 4–5)?

The NKJV reads: "All the kings of the earth shall praise You. . . . they shall sing of the ways of the LORD . . . ." The NIV reads: "May all the kings of the earth praise you. . . . may they sing of the ways of the LORD. . . ." The former better expresses the meaning of the text. "May does not express doubt but asks that the assured future may happen. The verbs could equally be futures: 'All . . . will.'"[1]

Knowledge of the ways of God (v. 6)? _____

_____

The promises of God (vv. 7–8)? _____

_____

WHAT DOES THIS PASSAGE MEAN?
(Interpretation)

1. What does it mean to praise God with a "whole heart" (v. 1)?

_____

_____

"We need a broken heart to mourn our own sins, but a whole heart to praise the Lord's perfections."[2]

CHARLES H. SPURGEON

2. How does David's response to his problems reveal a humble heart?

_____

_____

3. How might a proud person respond to the same kind of pressures?

_____

_____

4. How does God's treatment of the proud differ from His response to those with humble hearts?

_____

_____

5. David speaks of walking "in the midst of trouble" (v. 7). Why might God allow His children to be surrounded by problems? What does David experience in this desperate place that he might not otherwise have known?

_____

_____

HOW CAN I MAKE THIS PASSAGE A PART OF MY LIFE?
(Application)

1. Remember an occasion when you cried out to the Lord, and He heard you. What was the situation? Write a short note of praise to God, thanking Him for His deliverance.

_____

_____

2. Would God say that you have a proud spirit or a humble, lowly spirit? In what areas of your life do you struggle with pride?

_____

_____

3. David confidently says, "The LORD will perfect [complete] that which concerns me" (v. 8). (NIV: "The LORD will fulfill His purpose for me.") How does this promise encourage you?

_____

_____

"Our hopes that we shall persevere must be founded, not upon our own strength, for that will fail us, but upon the mercy of God, for that will not fail."[3]

MATTHEW HENRY

FOR FURTHER MEDITATION

Philippians 2:5–11

Responding to God

PRAISE

Praise God for what this passage reveals about His heart and His ways. Praise Him for His promises. Thank Him that all His purposes for your life will be fulfilled.

PRAYER

Confession: Admit any tendency you have had to take matters into your own hands and to fight your own battles, rather than relying on the Lord to handle the opposition and the pressure for you.

Supplication: Cry out to the Lord for strength and grace to face a difficult situation in your life.

Intercession: Use this passage as a basis to pray for someone whom God places on your heart.

SING TO THE LORD

Like a River Glorious

Like a river glorious is God's perfect peace,
Over all victorious in its bright increase;
Perfect, yet it floweth fuller every day;
Perfect, yet it groweth deeper all the way.

    Stayed upon Jehovah, hearts are fully blest—
    Finding, as He promised, perfect peace and rest.

Hidden in the hollow of His blessed hand,
Never foe can follow, never traitor stand;
Not a surge of worry, not a shade of care,
Not a blast of hurry—touch the Spirit there.

Every joy or trial falleth from above,
Traced upon our dial by the Sun of Love;
We may trust Him fully all for us to do;
They who trust Him wholly find Him wholly true.

                      FRANCES R. HAVERGAL

TAKE-AWAY THOUGHT

*What key thought, phrase, or verse from this psalm
will you take with you into your day?*

[1] *New Bible Commentary*, 578.

[2] Spurgeon, *Treasury of David*, 630.

[3] Henry, *Commentary*, 723.

Psalm 145

*P*reparing Your Heart

Ask God to quiet your heart and to speak to you through His Word. Ask Him to shine the light of His truth into your life. In this quiet moment, surrender yourself to Him and commit to obey whatever He shows you. Begin your time of devotion with this prayer:

> *Open my eyes that I may see*
> *wonderful things in your law.*
> *Give me understanding, and I will keep your law*
> *and obey it with all my heart.*
> *Show me your ways, O Lord,*
> *teach me your paths;*
> *guide me in your truth and teach me,*
> *for you are God my Savior,*
> *and my hope is in you all day long.*
> *Teach me what I cannot see;*
> *if I have done wrong, I will not do so again.*
>
> PSALM 119:18, 34; 25:4–5; JOB 34:32 NIV

*L*istening to God

- Read Psalm 145 thoughtfully and prayerfully.

- What key words stand out to you in this passage?

- Write out a key verse from this passage.

- Summarize the entire passage in a sentence or two.

WHAT DOES THIS PASSAGE SAY?
(Observation)

The ABC's of Praise

Each verse of this psalm begins with a different letter of the Hebrew alphabet. (Only one letter is missing; it would come between verses 13 and 14.) The first two verses and the final verse of the psalm form two "bookends" in which David expresses his desire and determination to praise the Lord. The verses in between list many reasons to praise and extol our great God. Psalm 145 is an introduction to the final collection of praises (Psalms 145—150). One commentator calls it a "high-water mark in the Psalter."[1]

1. How does David express both his personal relationship with God and his reverence and awe for God (v. 1)?

_____

_____

.How often does David praise the Lord? How long does he intend for his praise to continue (v. 2)?

_____

_____

> *"No day must pass, though ever so busy a day, though ever so sorrowful a day, without praising God. God is every day blessing us, doing well for us; there is therefore reason that we should be every day blessing him, speaking well of him."*[2]
>
> MATTHEW HENRY

.The theme of David's "alphabet praise" is the greatness of God (see v. 3). What does each of the following verses tell us is great about God?

vv. 1, 2, 21? _____

vv. 4, 5b, 6a? _____

v. 5a? _____

vv. 7a, 9a? _____

vv. 7b, 17a? _____

v. 8? _____

vv. 11–13? _____

v. 14? _____

vv. 15–16? _____

v. 18? _____

vv. 19, 20a? _____

v. 20b? _____

WHAT DOES THIS PASSAGE MEAN?
(Interpretation)

1. Circle every reference to verbal praise in this psalm (e.g., *speak, declare, tell*). Why is it important to speak the praise of the Lord to Him and to others?

_____

_____

2. Why is it so important to speak God's praise to the next generation (v. 4)?

_____

_____

3. The Old Testament contains many references that foreshadow the life and ministry of the Lord Jesus, who was yet to come. What connections do you see between each of these verses and the corresponding New Testament passage?

   v. 5 and Matthew 17:1–2

   _____

   vv. 6a, 11 and Matthew 8:26–27

   _____

   v. 7 and Luke 19:37

   _____

   v. 14 and Luke 13:10–13

   _____

   vv. 15–16 and Matthew 14:15–20

   _____

HOW CAN I MAKE THIS PASSAGE A PART OF MY LIFE?
(Application)

Using each letter of the alphabet, make a list of reasons to praise the Lord, including His attributes and His blessings.

A _____   M _____

B _____   N _____

C _____   O _____

D _____   P _____

E _____   Q _____

F _____   R _____

G _____   S _____

H _____   T _____

I _____   U _____

J _____   V _____

K _____   W _____

L _____   X, Y, Z _____

FOR FURTHER MEDITATION

Romans 11:33, 36; Revelation 4:10–11, 5:13

$\mathcal{R}$esponding to God

Today, focus on praising and blessing the Lord, rather than asking Him for anything. Read this psalm aloud, thoughtfully and prayerfully, one or two verses at a time. Personalize David's praise, and thank God for all His goodness and blessings.

SING TO THE LORD

Ye Servants of God, Your Master Proclaim

Ye servants of God, your Master proclaim,
And publish abroad His wonderful name;
The name, all victorious, of Jesus extol:
His kingdom is glorious, He rules over all.

"Salvation to God, who sits on the throne!"
Let all cry aloud, and honor the Son;
The praises of Jesus the angels proclaim,
Fall down on their faces and worship the Lamb.

Then let us adore, and give Him His right—
All glory and pow'r, all wisdom and might,
All honor and blessing, with angels above,
And thanks never ceasing, and infinite love.

CHARLES WESLEY

TAKE-AWAY THOUGHT

What key thought, phrase, or verse from this psalm
will you take with you into your day?

---

1 *Wycliffe Bible Commentary,* 550.
2 Henry, *Commentary,* 728.

SPECIAL THANKS TO . . .

Mark and April DeMoss, for providing a lovely mountain retreat where I could work on this project.

Jim Grissom, for your input on several of the psalms and for your prayers and encouragement.

Paige Drygas, for your editorial assistance and for your spirit that radiates the beauty and joy of the Lord.

My dear fellow servants at Moody Publishers, for your support in countless ways.

MORE INFORMATION

For more information about the ministry of Nancy Leigh DeMoss (*Revive Our Hearts* radio and conferences), or to order a catalogue of available resources, contact:

Revive Our Hearts
P.O. Box 31
Buchanan, MI 49107
Phone: (269) 697-8600
Fax: (269) 695-2474
E-mail: Info@LifeAction.org
www.reviveourhearts.com

Further Insights from Nancy Leigh DeMoss and Moody Publishers

A PLACE OF QUIET REST
Finding Intimacy with God through a Daily Devotional Life.

Have you found yourself fighting to make daily time with your Lord a consistent reality?

Author Nancy Leigh DeMoss shares from her heart and life how a daily devotional time can forever change your relationship with Jesus. She addresses common frustrations and pitfalls that most of us encounter in our devotional life, and makes practical suggestions for overcoming them.

"My dear friends book is so timely...so urgent. Its beauty in style and words will woo you to the feet of the Lover of your soul, and there teach you how to converse with the Sovereign ruler of the Universe. It will show you how to be still....to cease striving, to let go, to relax...and know that He is God. He has not left His throne." --Kay Arthur, Precept Ministries

ISBN-13: 978-0-8024-6643-3 , ISBN-10: 0-8024-6643-5 Paperback

MOODY
The Name You Can Trust
1-800-678-8812 www.MoodyPublishers.org

"Let the word of Christ dwell in you richly in all wisdom, teaching and admonishing one another in psalms and hymns and spiritual songs, singing with grace in your hearts to the Lord." Col. 3:16 (NKJV)

collection of thirty Old Testament Psalms read by Nancy
eigh DeMoss with a musical background.

or more information on Nancy's ministry and materials,
lease contact:

evive Our Hearts
O. Box 31
uchanan, MI 49107
vww.LifeAction.org